HENRY BLOGG OF CROMER

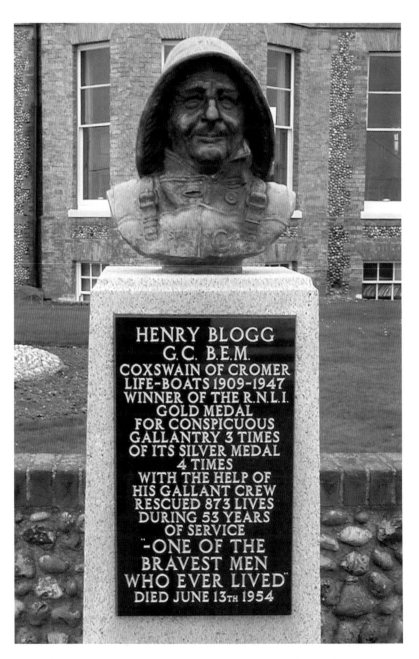

Bust of Henry Blogg outside the North Lodge council offices in Cromer.

Henry Blogg of Cromer

The Greatest of the Lifeboat-men

by

Cyril Jolly

POPPYLAND
PUBLISHING

First published in 1958 by George G. Harrap & Co. Ltd
Reprinted by Harrap 1974
Republished by the author twice
This edition published in 2002 by Poppyland Publishing, Cromer NR27 9AN
Reprinted 2007 (with updated information in the panel on page 23)

ISBN 0 946148 59 7

Designed and typeset in 10½ on 13½ pt Book Antiqua
by Watermark, Cromer NR27 9HL
Printed by Barnwell's, Aylsham

Pictures on pp. 190, 195 are by William Hickson
Pictures are also used by permission from the following collections:
Eastern Daily Press: pp. 215, 221, 225
Mrs Hilda Jolly: back cover (bottom)
Keystone Press Agency Ltd: pp. 60, 83, 213
Maritime Photo Library: pp. 63, 86, 132, 134, 137, 139, 141, 155, 174, 183,
211
Poppyland collection: pp. 3, 13, 15, 45, 48, 51, 68, 109, 123, 146, 149, 162,
177, 209
Poppyland Photos: p. ii, 80
Randall/Salter Magic Lantern Slide Collection: pp. 4, 31, 38, 79
RNLI: front cover, back cover

Contents

Map showing the position of wrecks mentioned in the book.

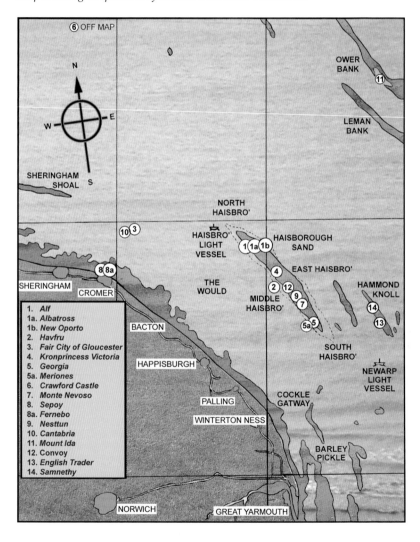

⑥ OFF MAP

N

W ─── E

S

SHERINGHAM
SHOAL

OWER
BANK

⑪

LEMAN
BANK

NORTH
HAISBRO'

⑩ ③

HAISBRO'
LIGHT
VESSEL

① ⑴ₐ ⑴ᵦ

HAISBOROUGH
SAND

④   EAST HAISBRO'

⑧ ⑧ₐ

SHERINGHAM

CROMER

THE
WOULD

② ⑫
⑨
⑦

MIDDLE
HAISBRO'

HAMMOND
KNOLL

⑭

⑬

⑤ₐ ⑤

1.   *Alf*
1a. *Albatross*
1b. *New Oporto*
2.   *Havfru*
3.   *Fair City of Gloucester*
4.   *Kronprincess Victoria*
5.   *Georgia*
5a. *Meriones*
6.   *Crawford Castle*
7.   *Monte Nevoso*
8.   *Sepoy*
8a. *Fernebo*
9.   *Nesttun*
10. *Cantabria*
11. *Mount Ida*
12. Convoy
13. *English Trader*
14. Samnethy

BACTON

HAPPISBURGH

PALLING

WINTERTON NESS

SOUTH
HAISBRO'

NEWARP
LIGHT
VESSEL

COCKLE
GATWAY

BARLEY
PICKLE

NORWICH

GREAT YARMOUTH

Preface to the new edition

Cyril Jolly's biography of Henry Blogg was first published by Harrap and Co in 1958, and was then reprinted by Harrap in 1974 and later by the author himself. We're delighted that Mrs Hilda Jolly has approved a new edition of the book, particularly as we approach the 50th anniversary of Henry Blogg's death and the bicentenary of the lifeboat station at Cromer in 2004.

We have taken the opportunity to make some minor amendments to the text, mostly of style, to reflect the years that have passed since the first edition. However we have endeavoured not to change the text so that it sounds as if it is written today – for instance, the reference to today's modern lifeboat at Cromer is still to the lifeboat *Henry Blogg*, which was retired from service in the town in 1966. A panel on page 23 gives some of the principal developments to the lifeboat service at Cromer since the first edition in 1958.

We have included a number of photographs not in the original edition where they help illustrate the story. We are particularly grateful to the RNLI for permission to use the two paintings associated with Cox'n Blogg, and to Adrian Vicary who maintains the Maritime Photo Library started by his father Philip. Philip Vicary faithfully recorded the lifeboat story at Cromer throughout much of the twentieth century. Wherever possible we have gone back to original copies of the photographs, but unfortunately it has not always been possible to find such prints. The photographs attributed to the Keystone Press Agency and the *Eastern Daily Press* have been reproduced from an earlier printing of the book; the publishers would be delighted to hear from anyone with original photographic prints of these pictures for use in future printings and at the Henry Blogg Lifeboat Museum.

Cyril Jolly wrote a number of books recalling aspects of Norfolk's history. We must all be grateful that he took the opportunity to interview men like Second Cox'n Jack Davies who had served with Henry Blogg from the last days of the nineteenth century through to the middle of the twentieth century. Hardly a month passes when some part of Blogg's story is not told in a local newspaper or national magazine article. Cyril Jolly's book is a key source for those stories and in it we know we are listening to men and women who were there with Cromer's greatest son – Henry Blogg of Cromer: The Greatest of the Lifeboatmen.

Author's Preface

There may be some truth in the saying that Norfolk people have one foot on land and the other in the sea. Certainly, I have spent many, many hours along its coast. But although I have known Cromer since I was a boy, it was not until a few years ago, when I was on holiday there, that I resolved, 'I will ask Henry Blogg if he will give me his life story.' I never did: he seemed such an immense figure – an Everest among men – that I dared not approach him.

My cowardice made no difference, for he would not have talked anyway!

Since then I have found out much about him from records and his friends – but I wish I knew what he thought about the big things of life. What strong current made him hazard his life a hundred times in the service of humanity? Was it ambition, bravado or a true love of his fellow men? Did he believe there was a purpose for the voyage of life and maybe a harbour below the horizon? I do not know and I doubt if anyone else does. He was clam-like on small things – how much more so on the things even talkative people rarely mention.

Certainly there were great depths to his character and although he was not a churchgoer, I believe Henry Blogg had a strong faith in God. I suppose it is hard to spend hours in a small boat far from land, with only the sea and the stars, without believing in

God. He said that Providence saved them on Hammond Knoll, but I am not sure if he knew where to look for comfort when life hit him so hard and so often. I do know that this Norfolk fisherman, who scoffed at ease and safety and gave the best of himself for sixty years to save life, was a big man. Apart from his daring and his leadership, his exemplary seamanship and his modesty, above all and beyond all, Henry Blogg was a truly noble man.

I wish to thank the Royal National Lifeboat Institution for permission to use reports in the *Journal*; E. P. Hansell, honorary secretary of the Cromer Branch RNLI, for access to local records; J. J. Davies, Tom Allen and Mrs J. W. Davies, of Cromer; Martin van der Hidde, of Rotterdam; Charles Vince, ex-publicity secretary of the RNLI; Alec Jackson, Henry Murrell and 'Jimmy' Dumble, ex-coxswain of Sheringham lifeboat, for their assistance.

I am indebted to the Norfolk News Company Ltd, for permission to use reports in the *Eastern Daily Press*, Sir Thomas Cook JP for reports in the Norfolk Chronicle, Rounce and Wortley Ltd, for reports in the *Norfolk Chronicle*, *Cromer Post* and A. C. Savin's *History of Cromer*. I am also grateful to George G. Harrap and Co Ltd, for the use of an extract from *Heroes of British Lifeboats*, by Gerda Shairer and Egon Jameson, and to Miss M. Caldwell, of Dereham, for reading the manuscript.

For the invaluable help so willingly given by Henry T. Davies, coxswain of Cromer lifeboat, and his wife I am more than thankful.

C. J.
Gressenhall, Norfolk
1958

1

The *Fernebo*

THE FIRST of a series of spectacular sea rescues which made the name of Coxswain Henry Blogg famous throughout the world was the service he and his Cromer lifeboat crew gave to the Swedish ship *Fernebo*.

Many a man has good reason to remember the winter of 1917, for it was one of the worst in the records. Tuesday, January 9, the day on which the *Fernebo* struck, was the worst of that terrible winter. A fierce gale, blowing at 50 miles an hour from the north-east, was pushing the waters of the North Sea on to the north Norfolk coast, making a perilous lee shore for shipping. It was just such conditions as these that had earned this part of the coast the nickname 'Devil's Throat', and had for centuries littered its shores with the bones of many ships.

Blinding squalls of hail and sleet had added further horrors to the fury of the wind and the sea. Throughout the previous night the gale had torn limbs from trees and slates from roofs and the hail had rattled like small shot on window-panes, as though challenging the inmates to leave their homes, while the dawn brought no relief.

Suddenly, above the noise of the storm, came the ominous burst of the rocket signal. No one was surprised, for this was 'lifeboat weather', and during the night both coastguard and Henry Blogg had been watching a small steamer, the Greek ship *Pyrin*, trying to ride out the gale in the roadstead off Cromer. Since daylight the coxswain had been to the top of the cliff two or three times, fearing, with good cause, that before long the ship would be in grave difficulty. Just after 11 a.m. the wind-buffeted watchers saw her run up the signal, 'Am drifting. Require assistance.'

As the townsfolk heard the rockets they shuddered at the thought of the crew of their lifeboat, the *Louisa Heartwell*, going out in such appalling conditions. A man did not have to be faint-hearted to flinch at those waves, which followed one another in fury to crash against the groynes with a violence that flung the tons of water skyward, only to fall back and add further to the confusion.

Before the sound of the second signal had died away some of the lifeboat-men were dashing towards the boathouse on the east gangway. They had to be off the mark as quickly as firemen, for a lost minute could mean a lost life. Some already wore their sea-boots; those who did not left it to their relatives to grab them up, fling a coat over their shoulders and bring them to the boathouse.

Before Henry Blogg reached the gangway he knew what a grim struggle lay ahead, for the tide was almost out and there were more than a hundred yards of difficult beach between his lifeboat and the water, where a fierce fight in a boiling surf was inevitable.

The ship in trouble was just two miles off Cromer. Not far, perhaps, on a summer day, but in the teeth of that gale, pitting oars against such seas, two miles was a very long way.

The boathouse was a tangle of men and equipment as the crew struggled into lifebelts and oilskins. Outside, forty willing launchers, including many soldiers billeted in the town, had arrived and were running out the ropes with which they would drag the boat across the sands. Others were taking up positions against the shafts at the rear of the carriage, to push the heavy craft into the sea.

The thirty-eight-foot-long *Louisa Heartwell* was of the Liverpool type. She was as big a boat as could be got on to a carriage,

The Louisa Heartwell, *a Liverpool class lifeboat, was Cromer's only lifeboat from 1902 to 1923 and was then at Cromer No 2 station for a further nine years. Henry Blogg was her second cox'n until 1909, when he became cox'n.*

but she was needed to work under sail to Haisborough Sands – twelve miles out. The lighter Norfolk-and-Suffolk type of boat, ideal where there was a rapidly shelving beach which enabled the boat to go straight into deep water, was no good at Cromer, where the violence of the surf on the flat beach made a light boat too dangerous to launch. The extra effort needed to get the big, heavier boat launched can easily be imagined. The *Louisa Heartwell* was, however, a fine boat and had done yeoman service at this danger-point to navigators. This was to be her great day – a day which would always couple her name with the *Fernebo* in what Commander Basil Hall, RNLI Inspector, called 'one of the most gallant rescues in the annals of the Lifeboat Service'.

Big as she looked in her house, the *Louisa Heartwell* seemed a puny thing against the breakers that were thundering on the shore. Her carvel-built hull looked wonderfully stout, yet those

3

The lifeboat house at the foot of the Gangway, from a hand-coloured lantern slide. The boathouse had been rebuilt to house the Louisa Heartwell *and was officially opened in September 1902.*

seas could crush her like an eggshell if they caught her unprepared. But she was game for the service – game as her crew and her launchers.

Led by the head launcher, Tom 'Bussey' Allen, the strong, eager men pushed and pulled at shafts and ropes and heaved at the wheel-spokes as the boat was set in motion. Shouting, laughing and swearing, Tom encouraged them as, helped by her own weight, the boat ran down the slope and on to the sands, where the launchers hauled and heaved like madmen in their effort to keep up her momentum.

There was not one launcher too many, for the wind checked the heavy boat and the wide iron wheel-plates of the laden carriage sank into the wet sand, demanding every ounce of strength the men could exert. It was a gruelling test, as there was a low bank of sand to be crossed and it looked as formidable as a range of hills. It was the first obstacle the sea had provided against the rescue of the men on board the *Pyrin*. Heaving and pushing with all their might, these stout-hearted launchers got the boat to the surf and the leading man on each rope was into the water, first to his knees and then to his waist. But before she could be got afloat a great wave caught and pushed her back, flinging the men on the ropes in all directions.

As the launchers again went deep into the water, with the salt spray half blinding them, they were pushed back once more and knocked sideways. They rallied and struggled on. Then, when the boat was at last deep enough to pull the launching-ropes and shoot her into the water and the crew were ready with oars poised, a huge wave flung her back again, scattering the launchers. Only by clinging to the ropes did many save themselves from drowning. Three times this happened, but suddenly the coxswain saw a chance and, taking their cue from him with skill gained by many a battle with the sea, the launchers snatched it and the *Louisa Heartwell* was afloat. The time was then about 11.40 a.m.

The second phase of the struggle was left to the crew of seventeen. Pulling with all their might, two men to each oar, they gained yard by yard, but could not prevent the wind and current from dragging them sideways towards a new danger.

Henry Blogg exhorted and instructed his crew, trying with every trick of seamanship he knew to counter that crabwise drift. But to the onlookers it seemed certain that the boat, so courageously launched, was doomed to be smashed against her own pier.

In groups on the cliffs, the promenade and the beach hundreds of shivering, rain-soaked men and women breathlessly watched the struggle. Then, when it looked as though only a miracle could save her, the *Louisa Heartwell* cleared the pier by a few yards. One could almost feel the release of tension as the townsfolk saw that another danger had been averted.

A smother of hail and spray hid the lifeboat for minutes on end and when the watchers, protecting their strained eyes with cupped hands, again saw the *Louisa Heartwell* she had hoisted a sail and was beating up towards the *Pyrin*.

The crew were barely conscious of the stinging hail, for the icy spray whipped up by the gale was flung continuously over the open boat. They pulled and pushed the heavy oars, jarred by each blow of the sea and thrown about by the steep pitching of their boat. At one moment they were climbing a great wall of water at an angle that threatened to shoot every man backward into the sea; the next, the boat had tipped into the trough of the seas, almost standing on her bows.

Progress was slow, but at 2 p.m., after three hours of back- and spirit-breaking effort, they had reached the *Pyrin*. The fine effort had its reward, for sixteen men were taken into the *Louisa Heartwell* and the stricken ship was left for the sea to toss contemptuously on the beach the next day.

The journey back to Cromer was much less strenuous, for with the roaring gale behind them they had to have the drogue out to steady them. Half an hour later they had landed the *Pyrin*'s crew.

The relief of the rescued at getting ashore was almost equalled by the relief the rescuers felt to be safely back after that gruelling contest. With their oilskins flapping in the gale, they clasped the hands of their friends as they ran into the surf to help in the landing. Then they made their way through the excited crowd to the boat-house, to shed their wet clothes, while Tom Allen, soaked to the neck, was organising the launchers to get the boat on skeats and then on to its carriage.

The crew were in an exhausted state, for the average age exceeded fifty and some of the members were nearly seventy years of age. Two and a half years of war had drawn away the younger men to the Navy and merchant fleet, leaving only the older men to man the boat.

But it had been a good day's work and now it was over they could relax and enjoy the steaming cocoa that brought back feeling to their numb bodies.

Their relief was short-lived, however, for hardly had they got into their dry clothes ready for the return home when a message came that the storm had put another ship in jeopardy. The Swedish ship *Fernebo* was in great difficulty three to four miles out.

The immediate reaction was that the Cromer crew could not aid her. They were too exhausted and some other lifeboat must go. Then came the news that the only other boats within reach could not be launched owing to the appalling conditions. Every effort had been made but all attempts had been unavailing. That meant that if help was to reach the *Fernebo* it must come from Cromer, or the crew would perish.

When he received the message Henry Blogg looked at his crew and knew that he must put it to them. In a few blunt sentences he told them how things stood. He was ready to go, he said and he believed his crew would want to go with him. The exhausted men saw the need and, tired as they were, battered as some of them had been, they were prepared to face that howling gale again. Even as they nodded or growled their readiness they knew that conditions were even worse than in the morning, for the tide was higher. But, having already achieved the seemingly impossible that day under Blogg, there was fire in their hearts. They would follow if Henry Blogg would lead.

They struggled back into their wet oilskins and cork lifebelts, tied their cold sou'westers under their chins and started the grim battle all over again.

The spirit of Cromer's lifeboat-men is shown in a dozen magnificent rescues while Henry Blogg was coxswain, but at no time did a crew show a finer spirit of sacrifice and duty than when those exhausted, ageing men faced that wild sea for the second time in a few hours.

On board the *Fernebo* two of the crew were attending to their thirty-two-year-old chief engineer, Johan Anderson, of Gothenburg, who had been injured when the steamer first got into difficulties. They brought him up from the engine-room to his cabin and were attending to his wounds when a heavy explosion threw them across the cabin. As, bruised and shocked, they scrambled up on deck to see what had happened there was a terrifying sound of rending iron and wood as the ship broke her back. The injured man was never seen alive again.

Entirely out of control and at the mercy of the storm, the Swedish ship had struck a mine. The explosion amidships split the ship in halves and as the onlookers watched they saw the two halves drift apart in a swirl of smoke and steam. Big seas tossed and hit them, but they neither listed nor sank, for the *Fernebo* was stacked with timber, which kept them buoyant.

Again there was no lack of launchers, for news that another vessel was in distress had spread through the town, and the shore and cliffs were soon lined with crowds of excited people ready to face hail and wind to see what they sensed would be a magnificent struggle. Warm homes and shelter from that Arctic wind were forgotten as they stood, soaked and shivering, look-ing down on Henry Blogg and his crew as they grappled with one of the worst seas they had ever known off Cromer. Even to this day old and middle-aged men proudly claim, 'I was there. I saw the *Fernebo*.'

As expected, the launching was worse than before and every effort seemed to be useless. The seas were so mountainous that even when the lifeboat was afloat the tired crew, with three fresh members, could not get her clear of the breakers. She was driven relentlessly back on to the shore, and wave following wave over-powered the oarsmen. One rearing sea caught the heavy boat as if she were a toy and hurled her right on to the beach. The sea had won the first round and the bruised crew sprawled half collapsed over their oars as the breakers continued their relentless pound-ing of the foreshore.

The men were helped by willing hands to the boathouse, while the *Louisa Heartwell* was dragged up the beach. The sense of defeat weighed upon them all, but they had done as much as human beings could do: the wild North Sea had proved too much for their strength.

While the coxswain and crew were making their second launching six men of the crippled *Fernebo* decided to risk getting ashore in a small boat. Their plight was desperate, for they did not realise the turbulence created by the huge waves which crashed unceasingly upon the beach. They could see that the

Louisa Heartwell was fighting a losing battle and decided that their only hope of survival was to take the desperate chance of reaching safety in their own small boat.

With bated breath the crowd watched the little craft leave the wreck and begin to move towards them. Such a suicidal attempt seemed sheer madness, but that tiny boat kept afloat as she crept slowly shoreward, aided by the force of water and the following wind. It was incredible! A miracle was happening before their eyes, for the boat had nearly reached the beach and had only a hundred, eighty, fifty yards to go to safety. Then, like a piece of driftwood, she was picked up and capsized and the six men were thrown into the seething water.

A cry of horror went up from the onlookers, but in an instant a dozen watchers on the water's edge, opposite the spot where the boat had overturned, linked hands and went into the surf. The leader, Private Stewart Holmes, was soon up to his waist, his armpits, his neck and was grabbing a struggling seaman. Another chain of men had formed to complete the rescue and between them they got the half-drowned man ashore. Even as they were doing this Holmes had reached and was pulling another man towards shallow water. A third, a fourth, a fifth and the last man was saved. Above the noise of the storm there arose cheer after cheer, for this was really something to shout about. A grim tragedy had been averted by the initiative and courage of ordinary folk who had acted without thought of their own safety. It was not known until later that the last seaman to be rescued had nearly drowned Private Holmes by his struggling and the soldier had to be hurried to hospital.

But the drama had not ended.

Through the spindrift and gloom of that wild day the rolling shapes of the two portions of the *Fernebo* could be seen as the storm drove them closer and closer to the shore. Then, about 5 p.m., they grounded, with the grinding roar of iron on stones. The after part struck the shore near the groyne, which runs four hundred feet into the sea below the 'Doctor's Steps'. The fore half was some hundred and fifty yards away against the next breakwater, opposite Cromer lighthouse. Fortunately the remaining crew were all on the after part of the ship.

The Cromer Rocket Life-saving Company set up their line-throwing gun opposite the wreck, but although this was only a short way out, the wind was too strong and the lines were blown wide or short of the objective.

The Sheringham Company also arrived and tried their skill, but with no better result.

By 9 p.m. the two companies had to admit defeat. Twelve rockets had been fired and not one had been near enough to be secured.

Two very powerful Army searchlights had been brought up from a near-by anti-aircraft unit and positioned on the cliffs and their beams directed downward clearly showed the plight of the remaining members of the *Fernebo*'s crew.

Here was drama indeed. The brilliant beams cut through the dark night and, illuminating the scene of the struggle, showed how near that broken hulk was to the shore and yet how far. The watching crowd could see only too clearly the terrifying turbulence of the sea filling that narrow gulf and making it almost impassable for men and boats.

The rockets having failed, the only hope of rescue now lay with Henry Blogg and his men. He had seen his exhausted crew rested a little from their six-hour battering and he realised that the sailors on the wreck would lose their lives unless he could do something quickly. He hurried to Commander Hall, who was in charge of operations.

The Commander was at first opposed to exposing the lifeboat and her crew to a further attempt under the prevailing conditions.

'It's impossible,' he said.

'No, it isn't, sir,' Blogg replied.

'But you won't get anybody to go out with you in this weather.'

'Oh, yes, I shall, sir.'

'Your men are worn out, Blogg.'

'It's not a question of my men, sir: it's the others – those who are in danger out there.'

'All right, Blogg, if you think so. And may God be with you.'

Blogg put it to his crew and although every man was feeling the strain, not one hung back or made excuses. Bruised and battered as they were by their previous attempt, they would try again to get those despairing figures off the wreck in the face of one of the fiercest gales Cromer had ever known. Compassion is a great driving force, but here it was being helped by confidence in a great and fearless leader. Wherever Henry Blogg led they would follow – even into the Devil's Throat.

On board the after part of the *Fernebo* Captain Evald Palmgren and the men with him could not see much of Cromer's lights, for the fear of Zeppelins had enforced a blackout, but they could see the dancing lights of many lanterns winking through the rain-swept darkness. Hope was almost dead, for again and again they had seen the flash of the rocket-gun and knew the wind was too strong for the projectile. The sea was now in its worst mood and showed no sign of abating. Everything seemed against them.

On shore, the news had gone round among the chilled watchers that their boat was going to try again and cheer after cheer of encouragement rang out across the water, bringing new hope to the wrecked men and voicing the challenge of the *Louisa Heartwell*'s crew flung in the teeth of that north-easter. The cheering could mean only one thing to the *Fernebo*'s men: a new attempt was to be made to save them.

Hope broke through the hardening crust of despair and they strengthened their grip on ropes and rails as the seas tried harder than ever to dislodge them.

So for the third time that day the boat was dragged on its carriage into the sea, this time in darkness, with the help only of swinging lamps, the light of which made the wet oilskins glisten and reflected back from the slanting, stinging sleet. For half an hour they struggled to get clear of the surf. Each time they tried they were swept back into the shallows, but each time they managed to keep the boat's head to the seas and start pulling again to get into deeper water. When half-way between shore and wreck the searchlights held the *Louisa Heartwell* as, for a moment, she rode the crest of a huge wave and, the next, was completely lost to view in the trough of the waves.

Some witnesses say five thousand people were gathered on the shore to watch that fight. Not one who saw it would ever forget it and many a man not used to praying did so now for that little boat fighting those mountainous seas. Wet through and shivering, they watched spellbound. Had that crew of twenty men all been in their thirties and fresh to the task they could not have pulled harder. It was magnificent. Henry Blogg was getting more out of them than they knew they had in them.

Suddenly a tremendous sea hit the *Louisa Heartwell*, smashing five oars and washing three more overboard and the boat began drifting almost helpless towards a groyne. Then, and only then, did they have to give up and Henry Blogg let the boat come ashore. Another round had been won by the sea!

A period of comparative inaction followed, during which the spectators stamped their feet and beat their arms to restore circulation. Some dashed indoors for a quick cup of tea or to snatch some food, but they were soon back on the shore, for what was happening in Cromer that night was something they might never see again, something they would have to talk about when stories of sea rescue were being told in the years to come. A county that boasted the greatness of its seamen was watching a trial of strength between some of its ablest lifeboat-men and the North Sea in a roaring fury. Neither the slashing hail nor the onshore gale that tried to push people from their vantage points above this arena could make them leave. They must see this thing through.

Rockets were still being fired, as though in a forlorn hope of reaching the wreck, and it was planned to wait until the tide ran out a little, then move the apparatus farther down the beach towards the ship. But Henry Blogg had seen a chance. The tide had reached a point where an 'outset', or seaward flow from a breakwater, was sweeping almost out to the wreck. If he could get the lifeboat in that it would help them to reach the ship.

The stern of the Fernebo *aground on the east beach at Cromer. Eighty-five years later her keel can still be seen at low water.*

'Tom Bussey,' said the coxswain to his head launcher, who had been wet through since morning, 'go and get them spare oars. We're going to have another go.'

That was the Blogg spirit – an invincible determination that would not let him see that he was beaten. For sheer courage Henry Blogg had no peer.

The men had had a breather. The new oars were shipped and scores of launchers ran the boat into the water for the fourth launch that day. Then, with searchlights focused on their target, they pulled with all their skill and strength.

Watched with agonised anxiety from wreck and shore, the lifeboat slowly approached the wreck and time and again it looked as though the stout boat must be flung against the barnacled sides of the broken *Fernebo*. One moment the *Louisa Heartwell* could be seen, vividly clear against the ship and the next she had slid into the trough of the waves and disappeared from view. No one could remember how long it took to get the exhausted survivors into the boat, but it seemed an age, fraught with anxious suspense, before the lifeboat began to draw away from the wreck.

Then, to the spectators' unspeakable relief, the victory rocket 'Green burns white' went up from the lifeboat and the searchlights followed her as she came quickly to the shore, where willing hands helped the eleven rescued men and the rescuers to safety.

It was nearly 1 a.m. and Henry Blogg and his crew had battled on and off for fourteen hours, risking their lives to save total strangers – Greeks and Swedes – from the fury of the sea.

It was over! Blogg had won the last round and beaten the North Sea in its worst mood. Overcome with joy after long hours of suspense and anxiety, the crowd shouted and cheered in wild excitement.

One Cromer man, looking back over nearly forty years to that scene, recalled how he had stood as a lad of nine watching the drama and although soaked to the skin had stayed far into the night to see the excited crowd drag the lifeboat ashore with her rescued men, her crew and her wonderful coxswain. He too had yelled himself hoarse acclaiming the lifeboat-men and there and then had placed Henry Blogg alongside Horatio Nelson and Robert Falcon Scott as his boyhood heroes.

If Nelson and Scott had stood on the cliffs that night and seen that service they would surely have made room for this humble fisherman of Cromer and his magnificent team, who had written one of the most thrilling chapters in lifeboat history.

The *Fernebo*'s crew were quickly got ashore and one man with severe scalds was rushed to Cromer hospital. Four others with minor injuries were also treated and then joined their companions at the Red Lion Hotel.

On the Thursday (January 11) of that week, when the gale had spent itself and the sea had sobered down, the body of Johan Anderson was washed ashore at Trimingham.

An inquest was held and Captain Palmgren identified his officer and told of his accident and loss and how he had gone on the 10th to search the wrecked forepart of the *Fernebo* to make sure he was not there. They buried the young Swedish seaman in Mundesley churchyard, close to the cruel sea that had taken this young life and then, as if in remorse, had given him up to be buried in consecrated ground on an alien shore.

Commander Hall, in a letter to the editor of the *Lifeboat Journal*, said of Henry Blogg:

> It was his own remarkable personality and really great qualities of leadership which magnetised tired and some-what dispirited men into launching and when the boat was launched it was the consummate skill with which he man-aged her and the encouragement he gave his crew which brought their efforts to such a successful conclusion.

For this magnificent rescue Henry Blogg was awarded the Gold Medal of the RNLI for conspicuous gallantry. It was the VC of the service – the highest award. The medals were presented at the Annual Meeting of the Institution at the Mansion House on

The crew of the Louisa Heartwell *wearing the medals awarded after the rescue of the* Fernebo. *Henry Blogg sits in the centre.*

April 17, 1917, at which HRH the Duke of Connaught presided. Before the medals were presented the Swedish Minister, Count Wrangel, handed over a cheque for £250 for the crew of the *Louisa Heartwell* from the owners of the SS *Fernebo*.

The Duke of Connaught also announced that, owing to his exertions and exposure that day in helping with the launching, Private Sharpe, of the Army Service Corps, had developed paralysis and there was little hope of his recovery. The Institution had granted him £100 and the Swedish Vice-Consul £25.

The second coxswain was awarded the Silver Medal and twelve members of the crew also received the Bronze Medal in recognition of their service to the *Fernebo*.

The station that had not won an Institution medal in sixty years had won fourteen in a single day.

2

The Setting

THE SHAPE of the north Norfolk coastline and the great storms that beat upon it make it one of the most dangerous and treacherous coasts for shipping. Winterton Ness is the most perilous point for mariners between the Thames and the Forth and Cromer itself was known to seamen for centuries as the 'Devil's Throat'. Norfolk, by sticking its neck out into the North Sea, asks for trouble – and gets it!

Cromer is so placed geographically that it is wide open to the sea right from the North Pole; and beyond, apart from one or two small islands and a corner of Russia, the seas continue unbroken to the South Pole. As an old fisherman said, 'There's hundreds o' miles o' sea rollin' on to this here coast.' And when the gale is from the north-east the power of the wind and the push of the waters make this a deadly lee shore.

During the year 1693 two hundred ships were lost in what was then called 'Cromer Bay'. If this sounds fantastic, let us remember that as late as 1866 nearly a thousand ships were lost on the East Coast in six months. These were, of course, mostly small coastal vessels bringing coal from Newcastle to London and southern ports and it did not need a great storm to sink many of them, for they were aptly called 'floating coffins', and too often earned that reputation.

Through the centuries the toll of vessels has mounted, until the charts of the north Norfolk coast are peppered with wrecks, making it a veritable graveyard of shipping. To counter the danger to the lives of the ships' crews, fifteen lifeboats were at one time stationed around the shores of Norfolk.

Yet, for all its perils, this sea-highway is an indispensable route to the port of London, the Humber and the Tyne and is one of the busiest in the world.

Thirteen miles south-east of Cromer lie the Haisborough Sands and although the Goodwins are called the 'Graveyard of Shipping', it is doubtful if they have claimed as many victims as these deadly Norfolk sands. The strong currents operating in the vicinity draw vessels on to them and once in the grip of the Haisboroughs few ships get free to sail again. The story of several Norfolk lifeboat stations is a fearful record of calls to ships caught in the moil of these submerged flats. One August morning during World War 2 the Cromer crew rushed out and gasped with horror to see six big ships, all within half a mile, dying on the sands with their backs already broken, although they had been stranded only a few hours.

The calls to the Haisboroughs were divided between Cromer and Palling after Winterton, Happisburgh and Mundesley had been shut down through lack of crews to man them. Then Palling was closed and with the most up-to-date lifeboats in the country and a slipway at the end of a pier enabling quick launches in the worst of storms, Cromer took nearly all the calls to the sands.

The impressive improvements in lifeboat design gave Henry Blogg a tool that was equal to his seamanship and spirit, for although he was no mechanic, he could handle a motor lifeboat with consummate skill. On several occasions when it was impossible to remain alongside a wreck by other means he maintained his position and took off the crew solely by using his engines and keeping head-on to the seas. Many times he ran his boat right over the flooded deck of a wrecked ship when no other method of rescue was practicable. He also stood by one vessel for four days and nights and he went thirty-two miles out to rescue the crew of the Mount Ida. None of these feats would have been possible with the row-and-sail boats that were in sole use at Cromer up to 1923.

But neither increased opportunities nor the craftsmanship of boat building provide the whole story. Given these to the full, there had still to be a Henry Blogg!

This coast of shoal and sandbank has known far more ample and spacious days. Blakeney and Cley were bustling with wool exports when Liverpool and Southampton were hardly known, and Cromer, Sheringham and Wells sent their fishing fleets as far afield as Iceland. The magnificent churches in most coastal villages are eloquent testimony to a prosperity that has long since departed. The decline has been partly the result of changing industries behind the ports, but also the changing ways of the sea. Norfolk juts out like a squat breakwater, collecting on most of its northern coast the beach material moved southward by wave action, so that Blakeney, Cley and Wells are now largely silted up, but Cromer and Sheringham are fighting against an ever-encroaching ocean. Like an insatiable monster, the sea is eating away the land in one spot and throwing back the undigested parts to build it up in another.

Every place from Sheringham to Pakefield can tell of vanished fields, cottages and churches; and towns like Dunwich and Shipden no longer exist. The coastline of Norfolk and north Suffolk loses two to three feet every year, for its soft gravel, clay and sand have little resistance to offer the ruthless invader. Give the North Sea half a chance and it will pour over the banks and far inland, as it did in January 1953, so that those who want to live here with the sea on their doorstep must fight with bulldozer and pile-driver, faggot and concrete, to keep it on the right side of their threshold.

Behind this wasting coastline runs one of Britain's most delightful coast roads. From Hunstanton to Yarmouth it dips and dodges through fishing villages and towns, with the sea on one hand and lovely undulating country on the other. Some of the finest churches in the land stand like sentinels on knolls overlooking this untrustworthy sea. Abbeys like Walsingham and

Binham, the ancient track of the Peddar's Way and magnificent halls like Holkham tell some of this insular county's story and are situated either on or near this lovely road. Here, too, is Cromer, the town that nursed and reared Henry Blogg.

Cromer is the most attractive resort of this attractive Norfolk coast. It lies nestling in wood, heath and hill, on the edge of the sea. You drop down to it from all directions and even then the town is not at sea-level, for there is a further forty or fifty feet by gangway or steps to the beach. The lighthouse stands guard on the east cliff, looking down on the town, and the pier with its pavilion and its lifeboat-house juts defiantly into the sea from the centre of the promenade. Above the mile-long sea wall rises the grass-covered cliff, with an imposing parade of hotels getting as near to its edge as they dare. Behind this multi-style frontage jostles a maze of fishermen's cottages, yards and sheds filled with fishing gear. This was the great coxswain's environment.

To Henry Blogg, returning from a lifeboat service, his home town looked like a mighty castle, with its ramparts built to protect the town from the sea's forays, rising from the water's edge, crowned by the magnificent 160-foot church tower of St Peter and St Paul.

Many of the older towns in Britain can trace their family history back to the Domesday Book, but Cromer can claim no such birth certificate. When the Domesday Survey was written Cromer was but part of the lordship of Shipden, or 'Shipedana' – a non-entity tucked away well back from the coast. But the invading seas gave Cromer a 'place in the sun' by gobbling up the more important Shipden. Faced with the ruins of Shipden's once flourishing port, the townsfolk of Cromer made hasty preparations to protect themselves from a similar fate.

By means of costly sea defences Cromer has been spared, but in five centuries the sea has advanced two miles. Shipden has now completely disappeared and is one of the lost ports of England. The lifeboat rides over its fields and the fishermen catch crab in its streets. A few old fishermen claim to have seen or touched with an oar the ruins of its church tower and some contend that the bells in the flooded belfry are occasionally rung by the motion of the waves. However that may be, at least one ship has been totally wrecked on it.

The inroads of the sea have caused many great cliff falls and although these have alarmed property owners, they have delighted geologists and archaeologists. Since 1746 Cromer has been noted for its Forest Bed deposits of the Pleistocene period and a thousand books and pamphlets have been written about them.

Even a respectable town like Cromer was not without its smugglers. In 1823 a party of bootleggers were surprised by Preventive Officers and a sharp fight ensued in which one smuggler was killed. In addition, Will Hotching, the renowned smuggler of Brancaster, was taught the trade – or craft – by a Cromer man. This tutor had a well-organised import business in tobacco, the goods being brought from Rotterdam in the stout ship *Harlequin*. The contraband was mostly sold to regular customers and the remainder hawked on a fish cart – under the fish. The trade declined about 1866, when Will Hotching was caught.

For a century Cromer has welcomed not only crabs to her crab-pots, but visitors to her beaches and she has shaped much of her economy around those folk who seek a quiet holiday in attractive surroundings, rather than the day-trippers who want a short stay to be a merry one.

Most visitors are not long in Cromer before they learn how proud the town is of its lifeboat station. They are soon told that its 1939-45 War record of 155 launches and 441 lives saved was the best in Britain and that one of its sons, born in a cottage on the cliff, became the most famous of all lifeboat-men.

Cromer's lifeboat story began in 1804, when the townsfolk, sick of watching helplessly while seamen drowned almost on their beach, called a meeting and subscribed £500 for a boat there and then. Twenty-five years later the Cromer branch of the RNLI was formed, just five years after the parent Institution. But it was not until 1857 that Cromer was taken over entirely as an RNLI station from the Norfolk Shipwreck Association. Since then its lifeboats have been launched 471 times and 1025 storm-threatened lives have been saved.

The old boat-house at the bottom of the east gangway now houses the No. 2 boat, *Harriot Dixon,* and the wooden-walled boat-house at the end of the pier shelters the forty-six-foot Watson-cabin-type *Henry Blogg*. Although it stands twenty-five feet above normal tides, on three occasions a north-easterly gale piled up the waters and flooded this boathouse, smashing the great folding doors to matchwood. Once it floated the lifeboat and banged her tail against her own winch as a further indignity. So now the *Henry Blogg* is chained down to prevent such insults.

The *Henry Blogg* is one of Britain's most up-to-date lifeboats – a gleaming, efficient lifesaver. Poised on her slipway above deep water, she has made some remarkably swift launches. On one service she entered the water four minutes after the first maroon had sounded. On another occasion the commanding officer of a Norfolk airfield reported a Meteor aircraft down 'in the drink', and eight minutes later he picked up his receiver and heard the coastguard say, 'Cromer No. 1 boat away, sir.'

In a century and a half there have been over a dozen lifeboats at Cromer. There have been unsuitable boats as well as good ones, but over those long years of storm and struggle designers and boat-builders have listened carefully to the reports of the men who used the boats, in an effort to find the best craft for local conditions.

The boat subscribed for in 1804 by Cromer's townsfolk was one of Mr Greathead's, in which the crew could get right up into the stern and bows. In 1845 they had a flat-bottomed boat with airtight decks, so that the bottom half of the craft formed one large air-tank. The second 'official' lifeboat was the self-righting *Benjamin Bond-Cabbell,* built by Beeching's of Yarmouth, in 1868. The fishermen, however, did not like this design, preferring a lower boat with greater stability. They asked for a change and said they would take their chance about capsizing. How right they were is shown by the fact that of the present fleet of 156 lifeboats only five are self-righting. So they got the *Benjamin Bond-*

Cabbell II in 1883. This was the craft in which Henry Blogg first served. She lasted until 1902, when the *Louisa Heartwell* took her place and won all hearts.

Cromer's first motor lifeboat, the Norfolk-and-Suffolk type *H. F. Bailey*, was launched in 1923, but a year later she was replaced by the more suitable Watson-cabin-type *H. F. Bailey II*. Meanwhile the row-and-sail boat *Alexandra* followed the *Louisa Heartwell* in 1931 and three years after she was superseded by the motor lifeboat *Harriot Dixon*. The *H. F. Bailey III*, which came

Publisher's note

Since Cyril Jolly wrote this book and its first publication in 1958, there have been many developments for both the RNLI and the Cromer station. The RNLI introduced the fast inshore lifeboats in the 1960s and undertook the replacement of all offshore lifeboats with faster vessels through the 1980s and 1990s. The Cromer record from 1958:

No 1 (Pier) Station:
Royal National Life Boat *Henry Blogg* (Operational No 840) 1948–1966
RNLB *Ruby and Arthur Reed* (ON 990) 1967–1985
RNLB *Ruby and Arthur Reed II* (ON 1097) 1985–2007
RNLB *Lester* (ON 1287) 2007–
(The pier lifeboat house was rebuilt in 1998–99.)

No 2 (Gangway) Station:
RNLB *Harriot Dixon* (ON 770) 1934–1964
RNLB *William Henry and Mary King* (ON 980) 1964–1967
D class Inshore Lifeboats 1967–

By April 17, 2007, Cromer's offshore lifeboats had been launched 999 times and saved 1642 lives; the inshore lifeboats had been launched 383 times and saved 97 lives.

in 1935, had the inestimable blessing of a Marconi wireless and could communicate with Cromer coastguard and Humber radio stations. She had a stability of 100 degrees, so that if rolled on her beam ends by heavy seas she could still right herself and this actually happened in the unforgettable service to the *English Trader*.

As Sir Godfrey Baring, chairman of the RNLI, said at the double naming ceremony in 1937, both the *Harriot Dixon* and the new *H. F. Bailey* were 'the best that money could buy and science devise. The Institution was glad to have them at Cromer, which they regarded as a model station.' That was not a fulsome compliment, but a genuine tribute to what Cromer had achieved in rescue work and efficiency.

That naming day was a proud occasion for Henry Blogg. A great crowd had gathered, the pier was trimmed with rippling bunting, the gleaming *H. F. Bailey* lay on the slipway, while the *Harriot Dixon* rode at anchor below her, curtseying gracefully to the swell. Then Sir Samuel Hoare broke the champagne bottles against the bows and the Bishop of Norwich dedicated both boats, saying, 'To the glory of God and the noble work of life-saving we dedicate these boats in the name of the Father, Son and Holy Ghost.'

As a land breeze carried these words seaward Cromer's coxswain stood looking across the familiar waters to the horizon, an upright figure in a reefer jacket, a man whose whole life was also dedicated to 'the noble work of lifesaving'.

In the ten years she was at Cromer, including the War years, the *H. F. Bailey III* justified her dedication. She blazoned her name on the record boards with magnificent services to the *Crawford Castle, Cantabria, Mount Ida, English Trader* and *Meriones*. In 1945 she handed over her work to the *Henry Blogg*.

3

The Man – Early Years

HENRY BLOGG lived all of his seventy-eight years in Cromer. He was born on February 6, 1876, in a cottage in New Street (now the Wellington Inn), on the cliff-top opposite the pier and almost in the shadow of the magnificent church. In summer young Henry would look out over a peaceful sea, with its wide semicircular horizon over which the sun both rose and set. In the distance he would watch the smoke-plumes of ships as they passed away out across this busy waterway. Then there were sailing-ships of all kinds, mostly colliers, and the hovellers from their own beach. These fascinated him especially as, with nose pressed against his bedroom window, he saw them coming back at daybreak, with their big brown sails set in a background of colour heralding the arrival of another fine day. He could see the dark shapes of the men as they moved about the boats, dropping the sails one after another as the boats neared the shore. And he particularly loved that last minute when, with sails down, the hovellers 'rallied' on a curling wave to come to rest with the scraping sound of iron on shingle and wet sand.

To landward he could look beyond the flint church tower to the green hills surrounding Cromer like the tiered seats of an amphitheatre.

Young Henry Blogg spent several years in the care of 'Granny' Blogg in Garden Street; then he moved to the home of his step-

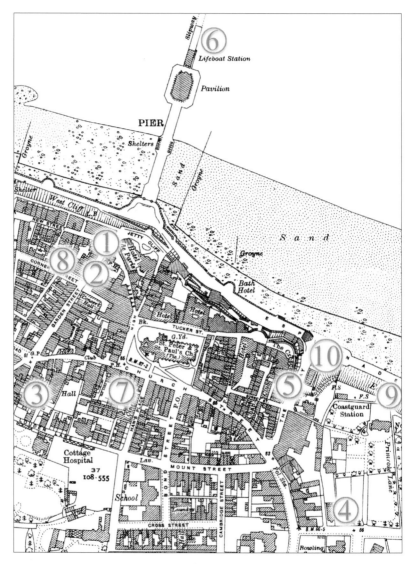

HENRY BLOGG'S CROMER *(based on the 1928 Ordnance Survey map)*

1 Birthplace

2 Granny Blogg's

3 J. J. Davies'

4 Goldsmiths' School

5 Gangway

6 Pier & 1923 lifeboat house

7 Swan Yard

8 Swallow Cottage

9 Blogg bust overlooking sea

10 1902 lifeboat house & museum

father, John James Davies, in Chapel Street, to be reared in the environment of a fishing family.

There were two other boys, John ('Jack'), eight years younger, and William ('Billy'), ten years his junior. There was always enough to eat – if only fish – and many long hours of hard work. For the menfolk there was danger and adventure and tragedy and humour – and always the sea. There were wet oilies, wet thigh-boots, the smell of fish and pitch and the talk was mainly of nets and lines and the bathing machines on the beach. But perhaps the thing uppermost in the minds of these simple people was the lifeboat service. Henry Blogg did not acquire its spirit – he grew up in it. His stepfather, John James, was second coxswain under his own father, old James Davies, who was in charge of Cromer's second 'official' lifeboat – the clinker built, row-and-sail *Benjamin Bond-Cabbell*.

Old James had been a member of the crew since 1863 and had been coxswain for four years when Henry Blogg was born. He took over from Cromer's first known coxswain, Robert 'Bully Bob' Allen.

As a lad Henry went to the Wesleyan Methodist Sunday School. Although most of the fishermen and their children attended a Nonconformist church, Cromer did not develop the strong fisherman-cum-Freechurchman tradition found farther along the coast. At Runton, 'Willie' Long, the 'saint in the blue gansey', became beloved for his character and his homely expositions of the fishermen who lived around Galilee. And at Sheringham, Henry 'Downtide' West, the lifeboat-man evangelist, was a typical fisherman-Salvationist and took a leading part in their famous 'Harvest Festival of the Sea'.

Henry Blogg went to the Goldsmiths' School on the corner of Overstrand Road. It had originally been founded as a Free Grammar School in 1505 by Sir Bartholomew Rede, a native of Cromer who became a Lord Mayor of London, and the Goldsmiths' Company rebuilt it in 1821. When Henry joined the school it had an average attendance of seventy boys and its master, John Hudson, was assisted by Alfred Salter. Goldsmiths' was a good school as schools went in those days. There were no frills, but a solid groundwork in many things that would stand the boys in good stead later on.

Henry was a good scholar. He learned quickly and then hung on to what he had learned. He was a spindle-shanked lad who never took part in games. He could not run and never learned to swim, but he would stand and watch other boys play, although he did not take part himself. Henry Blogg always seemed a little aloof from his schoolmates and was often the prey for bullies. He made but a poor hand of standing up for himself in a fight and in those rough days there were plenty of fights. Young Henry was frequently set upon by a smaller boy and even then made an indifferent showing. To his masters and those boys who were contemporary with him, there seemed little promise of a man who in a few years would become not only a lifeboat-man, but the finest coxswain in the history of the British lifeboats. No one thought then he would make danger his constant companion and outdistance the toughest of the young men in sheer endurance and stamina and would so master the craft of seamanship as to win world acclamation. But it was there – it must have been there – somewhere in that quiet make-up.

If he did not like fighting he liked getting aboard one of the coal ships when they lay on the beach and running over them and swinging from the bowsprit by a rope or dropping with a squelch into the wet sand.

His boyhood was rarely dull, but one of his most exciting days came when he was seven years old and his stepfather went out to the *Alpha* of Faversham.

On the night of October 3, 1883, a northerly wind increased until a strong gale was blowing, pushing up a heavy sea. The wind shook the windows and howled down the chimney of the cottage on the cliff. The seven-year-old boy lay in bed for hours listening to the thunder of the sea and the shrieking of the wind. He could not sleep, but tossed and turned, thinking of ship-wrecks, storms and lifeboat services. He was not the only one in the cottage kept awake by the storm, for 'Granny' could not sleep and close by his stepfather too stayed up very late, expecting a call. It did not come – at least, not that night. But at 2 p.m. the next day a schooner was observed flying distress signals eight miles north of Cromer and so the lifeboat was needed after all.

The 250-ton *Alpha* left Sunderland on Wednesday loaded with coal for Whitstable. At 8 a.m. on Thursday, about five miles north-east of the Dudgeon light-vessel, she shipped a very heavy sea. It damaged her, carried away her boats and severely injured one of the crew. She had struggled on her course, but in that wind and sea her condition became desperate and she hoisted signals calling for aid.

It was low tide when coxswain James Davies, with his son John James as second, tried to get away. The *Benjamin Bond-Cabbell* had to be pulled 200 yards over the sands and when they did launch her after a bitter struggle they could make no headway. After twenty minutes of frantic effort the lifeboat was flung back on the beach and they had to abandon the attempt. Young Henry, who was there to watch, nearly cried with disappointment.

The *Alpha*'s crew struggled frantically to claw off that lee shore, but she continued to come shoreward and appeared to be making for the old jetty. A man named Bosom 'Buz' Stokes jumped on a seat and waved excitedly, pointing westward. His signal was seen and the *Alpha*'s crew somehow managed to alter course so that she grounded opposite the marrams.

With the failure of the lifeboat the Cromer Rocket Brigade arrived and took up a position opposite the schooner. The first rocket was splendidly aimed and went right over the ship, but the crew could not secure it. The five drenched and desperate men on the wreck were huddled on the bowsprit and the seas were washing over the deck. The Sheringham Brigade also arrived, but no other line went near the ship, except the last, which was fouled by wreckage after it had been secured.

When the onlookers knew that the last rocket-line had been fired and the lifeboat also failed to get away the excitement and alarm reached fever pitch. The *Alpha* was going to pieces before their eyes and they were helpless to do more. The tide was rising and each wave was hitting her like a mighty hammer. Then the *Alpha* broke her back and both masts were carried overboard. Some of the falling tangle of gear caught Captain Reeve and swept him into the sea, but fortunately one of the crew managed to grab his jacket as he was washed past and drew him back on board.

The sea was scouring the ship's cargo of coal from the holds and this so lightened her that she lifted and bumped even closer to the beach – so close, in fact, that the distraught men could be heard above the sea's thundering, crying for ropes.

Darkness had fallen and a large tar-barrel was lit on the highest part of the marrams to illuminate the scene. Henry stood beside his grimly silent stepfather and the men of the helpless lifeboat crew and watched coastguard J. Davis courageously wade into the sea and throw a line. But it could not be secured and so, timing the breakers, he plunged into the sea and swam the rest of the distance with the line. This time it was fastened and one by one the six men used the rope to get ashore. Blankets were ready for them and they were then taken to the Red Lion. For his brave action coastguard Davis was awarded the Board of Trade's gallantry medal.

Captain Reeve and his crew attended church the next Sunday to give thanks for their deliverance. That did not end the story, for the failure to launch was the subject of much talk. Hasty charges of cowardice, which the vicar hotly denied from the pulpit, were brought against the crew and the Cromer branch held an inquiry in the old Fisherman's Rest Room. Captain the Hon. H. Chetwynd, chief inspector of lifeboats, and many leading townsfolk and fishermen were present.

James Davies described the efforts after launching and said it had been utterly impossible to row against such a strong wind and sea. Others of the crew endorsed his statement and Captain Chetwynd said that from his inquiries he believed it was not humanly possible to have launched in such conditions.

Then came the men's complaint that the lifeboat was not suitable for Cromer and James Mayes, a fisherman, produced a model,

The wreck of the Alpha *on the west beach at Cromer. The rowing lifeboat had not been able to launch through the heavy breakers on the beach.*

made by Samuel Simons for the Great Exhibition of 1851, of the boat then in use at Cromer, which allowed the crew to get right up into the bows and stern. Most of the crew favoured a return to this type of boat. Captain Chetwynd advocated the self-righting type, but the fishermen called these boats 'roly-polies'. As they were the men who had to take the boats out and whose lives were risked in her, the RNLI listened to their views and a year later the crew got the type of boat they wanted. She was given the name of the old boat – *Benjamin Bond-Cabbell* – and the type became known as the Cromer type, although only a few were built.

As top boy of the top form when eleven and a half years old Henry Blogg had little reason to remain at school and his step-father had need of him in the crab-boat. So young Henry left

Mr Hudson's school of reading, writing and arithmetic for his stepfather's school of baiting, hauling, rowing and seamanship. It was also a move into Form II in the school of life.

It seems a tender age to take a small oar, or paddle as it was called, and take up the hard life of a fisherman, but it was the accepted thing in those days for a boy to leave school at that age, or even earlier, and start working.

So Henry Blogg took his place in the boats and learned to use an oar and handle a sail; to bait the cod-lines with mussels, crab-pots with gurnards and whelk-pots with herring or fish offal. He was taught to keep a 'north eye' open for the weather changes even at the busiest time of hauling or shooting the lines and handle an open boat in the surf and among the sandbanks off the Norfolk coast. Tides, currents, rocks, shoals and all the lore of his craft had to be acquired and a box on the ears drove home many a verbal instruction! If he had learned well under Mr Hudson, Henry also learned well and eagerly under his stepfather. The knowledge gained was put to such good use in his rescue work that it was truly said of him, "He knew what his boat could do and as nearly as a man may what the sea could do." His heart was not in being a farm-worker, a clerk, or a bricklayer; he wanted to be a fisherman as good as John James Davies, his step-father.

Henry Blogg became one of the finest of a fine breed of men – the longshore fishermen. On them the lifeboat service depends and it is a tragedy on the East Coast, at least, that they are disappearing faster than we like to think. When Henry Blogg was unanimously elected coxswain of the Cromer lifeboat there were sixty fishermen present, with eighty to a hundred boats on the beach; today twenty could not be mustered, with only half a dozen boats. The longshore fisherman is disappearing fast because of the steam trawlers. Working far out to sea, they have taken the bulk of the cod catch and now the longshore fisher-man can earn little in the winter and not enough in summer and autumn to keep him through the year. When Henry Blogg was a young man and long since, there were herring and mackerel in autumn and from November to late January plenty of cod. Now there are hardly any cod and very few herring or mackerel. So along the coast where each stone-built fishing-village had formerly its score of fishermen with a little fleet to-day there are a couple of boats, or, more likely, none at all – and certainly not enough fishermen to man a lifeboat.

The year that Henry Blogg changed his hard school seat for a hard and wet seat in a crab-boat he saw a most unusual sight – a ship wrecked on a church!

It was the excursion steamer *Victoria* of Yarmouth with over a hundred passengers on board which struck the remains of Shipden church, or 'Church Rock' as it is called, just as she was leaving Cromer, having picked up her passengers.

August 8, 1888, was a fine day for a sea trip and the *Victoria* moved off smoothly over a shining blue sea. A fisherman shouted as he saw the ship moving away, 'She's going towards the rock,' but they did not hear or heed. He told afterwards how a few days earlier at low tide he had leaned out of his boat and, with an oar, touched the rock.

There was a grinding jolt that flung the passengers in all directions and badly holed the ship. Water poured in to increase the terror of the screaming women passengers and the Victoria settled on the rock. They lowered the *Victoria*'s boats at once and several fishing-boats rushed out to assist. The hundred passengers were transferred and all movable stores gradually brought ashore in salvage trips. The grumbling, flustered passengers went home by train with an understandable grudge against seaside churches.

Young Henry and other Cromer lads watched with fascination the attempts to salvage the uninsured *Victoria* by means of a traction engine on the cliffs. A hawser was taken out and fastened to the wreck, but the distance was too great and the engine could not pull out the slack. The hawser parted two or three times. Had the engine gone on to the beach and been much nearer and level, it might have dragged the ship ashore and the remains of Shipden church with it. As it was, the Trinity House authorities decided the wreck was a danger to navigation and blew it up – and some of the church rock also!

In the little cottage in Chapel Street there was a noisy, growing family. Jack and Billy both went to the Goldsmiths' School when old enough but were not so adept with pencil and slate as Henry. A few years later they came under the same schooling in seaman-ship from their father as Henry had received and both became outstanding members of the Cromer crew, winning many dis-tinctions and helping to push their station to the top of the 'Life-boat League'.

Fishing runs in families and the craftsmanship as well as the gear is handed down from father to son. There are families of longshore fishermen along the Norfolk coast today whose names were known there a couple of centuries ago – the Peggs, Wests, Craskes, Coopers, Middletons, Allens, Harrisons, Coxes, Davies and Bloggs. At one time the Cromer lifeboat was predominantly Balls, then Allens; and then a few years later there were nine Davies in a crew of twelve.

With the three able boys to help, John James Davies kept three boats – the *John Roberts*, the *Britannia* and the *Boy Jack*. He also kept the three boys out of mischief by giving them plenty to do. They should have been very good boys if there is any truth in the saying that 'the devil finds work for idle hands to do,' for their hands were never allowed to be idle except on the Sabbath Day. Games and leisure were not in John Davies' curriculum.

With the first warm days of March, John James began looking at the blackthorn bushes for signs of buds. He just itched to get out his crabbing gear and as soon as he received his cue from Nature he had the boys bustling with crab-pots, lines and buoys and the fever of crabbing seized them all. As the temperature of the water rose the crabs left their winter quarters to feed, but the fishermen could not bring ashore all that found their way into the crab-pots. There were regulations about size; and 'white feet' crabs, which are not so meaty as 'black toes', could be sold only after the first week in July. That week was usually a bumper one – a crabbing harvest!

In mild winters crabbing often went on right up to Christmas, but in late July, August and September the men helped out the women with the beach trade – huts, chairs, tents and towels. This was also augmented by longshore herring fishing in the hovellers during September and October. From November to January there would be long lining for cod; and from January there was plenty of work repairing nets and crab-pots and overhauling boats. This lasted until crabbing began again.

Cromer crabs were famous before their lifeboat. Crabs like a hard sea bottom and lie close inshore. The ridge of rocks jutting out a mile and a quarter opposite Cromer lighthouse is a crab's, if not a seaman's, idea of paradise! They are caught in 'pots' – a cast-iron grid bottom for weight, with a curved frame of hazel supporting a net. A tunnel of braided twine allows the crab to enter for the bait and once inside he cannot get out, unless the net has just one small fracture and that will be sufficient for him to side step away to freedom.

Whelks seek more comfort than crabs and choose a cosy clay bottom for their beds. That means that the Cromer fishermen have to go three miles out to find them and entice them into whelk-pots made from an iron frame netted over. Twenty-five to thirty pots are strung out in a line, or 'shank.'

When cod were a paying proposition at Cromer they were caught with lines of hooks baited with whelks or mussels. Each line, or 'long pack', carried 400 to 450 hooks and a crab-boat carried six 'long packs'. The lines were laid just before dusk, seven or eight miles out, and hauled at daybreak. It was a long pull with a laden boat and tide or wind against them!

When the short and sharp mackerel season begins Cromer fishermen try to make their harvest by crabbing in the daytime and mackerel-fishing at night. It means a double haul – and also non-stop working. When Henry, Billy and Jack were partners they twice went from Monday morning until Saturday night, crabbing by day and mackerel-fishing at night. During that time they did not take off their clothes or go to bed. When Saturday night came and they sat down to share out the takings, two of them fell asleep at the table. The share-out had to be left until they had all had a good sleep. Jack Davies recalls with a grin that the week's takings were nearly £30.

The bathing-machine business was profitable and less laborious than fishing and often more entertaining! Even so, it was not all done at a booking-desk. The machines had to be drawn up and down the beach according to the tide, so that the Victorian ladies could step daintily straight from the steps of the machine into the water. Horses were used to pull the heavy machines. Henry Blogg was employed as a lad on this work and at one time there were a hundred machines to be moved. It was hard work for the horses and Henry kept them at it; but when it was over he always cared for them well.

The contrast in bathing-costumes between those days and the present brought many a humorous comment from Henry Blogg, especially when he told how, when certain titled ladies bathed, one of the fishermen was employed swimming fully clothed to seaward in case anyone got into difficulties.

The firm of J. J. Davies and Sons had a hut at the bottom of the east gangway and there Henry Blogg would do the letting, also supplying on hire, from a large hamper, rough towels at a penny and bathing-dresses at a penny.

In the winter the men worked in a shed repairing 'pots'. The nets that cover the framework were braided by hand and Henry Blogg held the record for many years by braiding a crab pot net in thirty-five minutes. That record has since been beaten, but it showed that Henry could do little things well and big things very well.

The hovellers, which were largely used then, have almost disappeared from the villages of the East Coast. They were larger than the crab-boats and could be taken far out to sea to brave some of the worst weather the North Sea could throw against them. They were fine boats for the work, clinker-built, with a large brown sail on a short mast. In the bows was a rough caboose, or 'cuddy'. There was a small tortoise-stove, an oil lamp and a table – not elaborate but useful fittings. The men kept their oilies and belongings in the 'cuddy' and prepared their primitive meals. If there were four men in the hoveller, they could take turns to get a little sleep in this cramped cabin. Even in good weather a fishing trip in a hoveller offered few comforts.

In 1894, when Henry Blogg was eighteen, he became a member of the lifeboat crew. For six years he had been fishing with his stepfather who, the previous year, had become coxswain of the *Benjamin Bond-Cabbell II*, as old James had died shortly after being struck under the heart by the lifeboat tiller, in a rough sea. The same year that Henry Blogg put on his cork lifebelt and woollen 'pirate' cap, John Davies was presented with the medal of the Royal Humane Society for saving life.

When times were hard in the fishing-villages most fishermen were keen to supplement their earnings by a lifeboat service. So many men ran for the boathouse when the alarm was given that the rule was made that only those who got a lifebelt could go. Three belts were reserved for the coxswain, the second coxswain and the bowman and there was many a tussle for the others. On one occasion a fisherman whipped out a knife and started to cut the belt in half, crying to his competitor, 'If I can't have it, then you shan't. So we'd better halve it!'

In order to arrive early and make sure of a belt, some men dashed half-dressed to the boathouse and more than once a man has been seen pedalling furiously towards the beach wearing only his trousers. His relatives followed, presumably, as quickly as they could with the rest of his clothes! 'Never volunteer for anything' is the principle adopted by 'old soldiers' in the Forces, but that was the only way into the lifeboat service. It was a job for volunteers. It was not every man who felt he could drop whatever he was doing at the crack of the maroons and run to the boathouse. Some who did volunteer were not accepted, as it needs more than courage and more than brawn – the service demands sacrifice. In no other service is the true brotherhood of man more clearly shown, for the call comes, not to save one's relatives or friends, but to risk life itself for the sake of utter strangers. Even our country's enemies demand that you break

The second lifeboat at Cromer to carry the name Benjamin Bond Cabbell – *the first lifeboat in which the young Henry Blogg served.*

your back and burst your heart to save them. The qualification is not colour or creed but need and if a man will risk his life and his livelihood to answer the call, then, however foul-mouthed or brutal he may be, there is something fine in him.

John Davies did not have to threaten or cajole his stepson into taking a belt. The risks and rigours were no deterrent to Henry Blogg, for the sea was in his blood as surely as it was in the blood of Lord Nelson, Admirals Sir Cloudesley Shovel, Sir John Narborough and Sir Christopher Myngs, who all belonged to this north Norfolk coast. And if the sea was in his blood, so was the lifeboat service. He wanted to join long before he was strong enough to take a man's place in a boat. The success of each venture, however, depended not on engine-power but on the skill and power of the oarsmen and he was eighteen before he was allowed to take a belt.

It was a big day for Henry Blogg, when he first tied on his sou'wester with the letters RNLI on it. Now he could study first-hand the technique his stepfather so often talked about at meal-times and during the long pulls to the fishing-grounds.

There was another big event in Cromer that year, for the east promenade and wall were built; and the only access to the beach, the east gangway, was almost as busy as the Strand with carts bringing material and men doing the work.

Although Henry Blogg joined the lifeboat in January, it was December 28 before he saw his first service – to the *Fair City of Gloucester*.

The ship had got into difficulties in the north-west hurricane blowing that Friday. The north and north-west are the worst quarters for shipping off the north Norfolk coast, as – apart from the wind danger – the tides are stronger. When the vessel was four miles off Cromer her masts were carried away and Captain Armitage, realising the danger to himself and to his crew of three, burned many flares, hoping the coastguard would see them.

The flares were seen, the alarm sounded and – just before midnight struck in Cromer's church tower – the *Benjamin Bond-Cabbell* was launched into an ugly, life-seeking sea. There were squalls of rain and hail and it was so cold that young Henry might well have had his ardour chilled for ever.

The seventeen men pulled and strained at the oars, battling against the angry sea and, after ninety minutes' gruelling toil, they found the ship with her anchors mercifully holding.

Rightly, Captain Armitage was unwilling to leave his ship. He thought if he could hold out till daylight he might get a tow into port from some passing steamer. John James Davies, the coxswain, thought it wise to stand by the vessel. Through sleet, hail, wind and seawater he did so until 4.30 a.m., with his crew, including young Henry Blogg, chilled to the marrow. Then, attaching a hawser to the lifeboat, the *Fair City of Gloucester* weighed anchor and both were driven southward, in company, through the wild December night towards the shore. It was a chilly initiation for Henry Blogg.

Most people who knew Henry Blogg knew he did not smoke or drink, but not all knew why. It was the practice when Henry was young to share out the lifeboat rewards in a public house, going round each house in turn. Some of the share-out often returned the same evening over the counter to the publican. On the evening Henry Blogg took his first share he too parted with some of his earnings and received more liquid refreshment than he had ever taken before.

It was very late that night when he got home and his step was anything but purposeful and firm. His stepfather and brothers heard him coming and chuckled, 'Henry's drunk'.

But after Henry had got to his bedroom, he called out in a thick voice, 'S'all right, I'm not drunk.'

Next morning the young lifeboat-man had a thick head, sour mouth and an unsettled stomach. He said to John Davies that day, 'Never again.' And it was never again! In the years that followed he was asked a thousand times to 'come and have one,' but he never wavered from his resolution.

When he started to smoke he lit his first cigarette on the cliff and walked down to the front. A friend, noting the cigarette, asked him what it felt like. He said, 'I feel like a pig with a straw stuck in my mouth.' That was Henry's first cigarette. It was also his last.

It was while Henry Blogg was attending to bathing machines and hut-letting that he became attracted by Ann Brakenbury. They had known each other for many years, for Ann was a Cromer girl, just two years younger than Henry. She was employed letting beach-chairs – the sort with iron frames and wooden slats for seats. They typified that prim era, but would hardly suit our idea of a comfortable lounge in the sun.

When Ann's brother Charlie was asked if he knew how the courtship started he just smiled and said, 'Well, you know, that sort of thing's catchin'.'

Henry and Ann had much in common, apart from beach-chairs and huts. There was no wide difference of class or wealth between them and no language problem, for they both spoke the Norfolk dialect. They had secluded paths to follow along the cliffs and through the woods that surrounded Cromer. There was the sea, with gorgeous sunsets over Sheringham Shoal and the moon shining on smooth, unruffled waters. They listened to the murmuring gossip of wavelets on the shingle and the constant sound of water in motion, the onrush of a powerful wave and the hiss of foam as the waters drained back to the sea to check the next rank of eager invaders. The sea, that was to show its cruelty a hundred times to the lifeboat-man, showed them a gracious face.

They walked along the shore arm in arm, a score of times passing the spot whence in coming years the young man was to win world-wide fame by his seamanship and daring. They raced one another up the cliff paths and sat on the cliff-top near the old lighthouse, watching the gulls skim the smooth surface of the water with effortless grace. They watched the white clouds pass overhead and drift out to sea. They noted the changing colours of the water, the fretted edge of creamy waves and the ominous patches of white foam where the sea broke on the hidden rocks.

They talked of generous visitors and haughty visitors, of snubs and compliments, of ugly roker fish and storms and wrecks. Then, as their love deepened, they talked of a little cottage of their own, tucked away from the east wind but open to the sun and with a window to the sea.

They made their little plans and schemed their little schemes, on the edge of the eternal sea. While the country discussed the fluctuating fortunes of the Boer War and the wonderful old lady who was Queen of England, they talked of tables and chairs and a smart, brass-knobbed, black iron bedstead.

Rev. A. Selwyn, vicar of Cromer, married the young couple in the parish church on October 18, 1901. Ann looked attractive, Henry smart and pleased with himself in his reefer. And there at the altar they made their vows and began a partnership that only death broke nearly fifty years later.

They did not go away for a honeymoon, for that was a luxury they could not afford, but they settled into their cottage in Chapel Street and to them the world was very fair.

Ann was twenty-three and Henry two years older. They had their ups and downs, but for half a century they made and kept their home and their loyalties. Ann was a good wife, keeping a spotless house and showing her industry in Henry's clothes. She knitted his 'ganseys' and boot-stockings and no one ever saw him in a dirty slop or with a hole in a woollen garment. She was a good plain cook, attempting nothing fancy, but serving with pleasing variety the things that Henry liked. She kept a good table, pheasants and fowls being frequently served, not because they were cheap or easy to get, but because they pleased Henry. And when he reached home after a gruelling contest with wind and weather there was hot food and drink for the exhausted man.

Although Ann Brakenbury was nervous and 'on edge' before visitors, she became a tower of strength in times of duress – especially in the War years, when the strain imposed on Henry Blogg was terrific. Only those very close to the pair knew how much weight she took off his loaded shoulders.

Although Henry Blogg hardly ever left Cromer, except to receive a decoration or to see Cromer Town Football Club play in a final at Norwich City's ground, the Nest, or Carrow Road, Ann had even fewer outings; but she did go to London once in the nineteen-thirties to see her man decorated at the Mansion House. That was all. For the rest, there was the housework, the long hours of waiting through storm-racked nights and the intense pride in Henry's successes. That pride was touching in its devotion. She saved little pieces of wrecks, even a jar of sand that her husband scooped up from the Haisborough Sands.

They looked tawdry to the casual visitor, but to her they were precious because they were connected with Henry.

Nearly a year after their marriage, on September 26, 1902, a son was born and Henry Blogg was the proudest man in the kingdom. He was always a family man, loving home life and centring his affections and confidences almost entirely in the family. Moreover, he loved children and now he had a son of his own, a son he could teach the ways of the sea, who would grow to manhood to take a place with him in the crab-boat and, perhaps, in the lifeboat.

No one will ever know what plans he wove around the little head; what hopes he had; what dreams he cherished. But they were not to be. One of the hardest blows that life was to deal him came when the boy he had so proudly named Henry James died before he was two years old and it was not until December 5, 1907 that Henry and Ann had their second child Annie Blogg, called by them 'Queenie'.

In the year his son was born his stepfather, John Davies, retired from the lifeboat through ill health. He had been coxswain for nine years. James 'Buttons' Harrison took his place and the man they chose as second coxswain was Henry Blogg. At a time when there was much vying for the responsible jobs of the crew he had become second-in-command at the age of twenty-six and after only eight years' service. It seems evident now that the qualities that were to be so clearly marked later had already appeared and men who would pass quick censure for weakness but give ready acknowledgement of ability elected him to the second place in their crew.

Although reticent and unsociable in so far as he was a teetotaller, Henry Blogg was popular, for he was a kindly man, unwilling to hurt his fellows by word or deed, and he was just.

He might have been out of favour for not indulging in a beard, for in an age of 'face fungus' he remained clean-shaven. He did not shave himself but regularly patronised a Cromer barber. He got an awful shock during the Second World War when notices appeared: No Shaving through Shortage of Staff. After sixty years, Henry Blogg had to shave himself. He bought a safety razor, but the term 'safety' misled him and he managed to cut himself in a score of places. After his first shave he looked as though he had been peppered with buckshot!

Henry Blogg was second coxswain for seven years and while

under 'Buttons' Harrison the *Louisa Heartwell* made ten fine services, saving eighty-two lives.

One rescue which the secretary reported as 'promptly done' was to the *Zuma*, seventy-nine tons, of Wisbech. It took place on September 17, 1906. There were nine people on board, including the Captain's family, two of them girls. The *Zuma* was bound from Leith to Sandwich with a cargo of coal and was struggling off Cromer against an east-north-east gale that was piling up heavy seas when she sprang a leak. Her sails, too, were blown away. Almost unmanageable, with water rising fast in her hold, the crew worked like demons at the pumps to keep the ship afloat and the two girls took their places with them.

Cromer's coastguard, who had kept a paternal eye on the *Zuma* for a long time, reported she was in trouble and flying a distress signal. It was then 7.30 a.m. and within thirty minutes the lifeboat was away. They took on extra crew to double-bank eight oars, but even so it took an hour to reach the wreck. The *Louisa Heartwell* took off the nine persons and then stood by through the rest of that day and night, having put eight members of the crew on board to keep the pumps going until a tug, which was expected from Yarmouth and which, apparently, took an age to reach them, finally arrived. They then assisted the crew to get the boat to harbour.

It was 4 p.m. on the 18th when the lifeboat got back to Cromer and a large number of visitors had gathered to see the men return. They had been over thirty hours at sea.

Most North Norfolk fishermen not only bear the name their parents gave them but one their friends have added. The nickname may give little indication of the bearer's character but it is a useful method of distinguishing members of the same family bearing the same Christian name. Where there are large families in small fishing communities and the parents have proudly passed on their own names to the children, identities become mixed. The stranger asking for Jimmy Davies is confused when he is told there are four at Cromer, or six Bob Wests at Sheringham; but if he asks for 'Old Joe' Davies or 'Teapot' West, all is well.

The Louisa Heartwell lifeboat is wheeled down her ramp to the beach from the 1902 lifeboat house.

At one time the *Louisa Heartwell* not only carried an efficient crew, it also bore an amusing medley of nicknames: G. 'Buckram' and H. 'Butler' Balls; T. 'Bentley' Kirby; G. 'Crow' Rook; G. 'Mus' Cox; W. 'Kite' and W. 'Will Doll' Rix; S. 'Baby Sam' and H. 'Loady' Nockels; H. 'Ry' and R. 'Young Dinger' Blogg; J. 'Old Sailor' and G. 'Sailor' Allen; G. 'Measles', W. 'Ponsey', J. 'Kelly', J. 'Jimmy Buttons' and W. 'Billy Buttons' Harrison; W. 'Captain', R. 'Lantern' and J. 'Old Joe' Davies.

The earliest-known honorary secretary was W. G. Sandford; then came George Rust. F. H. Barclay, who served twenty-six years, took over in 1908. It was in the same year that the Institution honoured Cromer station by choosing it to demonstrate lifeboat launching and handling to a Netherlands Royal Commission on Life-saving. Henry Blogg's first service in charge of the *Louisa Heartwell* was on December 19 of that same year. They were called out to the smack *Marcus* of Lowestoft, which had been seen burning flares. She had grounded on Haisborough Sands and had begun to leak badly.

After a cruelly difficult row of thirteen miles, they found no vessel, so went to speak with the captain of the lightship and were told that the crew of the smack had been picked up by her and had been taken off by the Palling lifeboat. The Palling boat, being nearer to the wreck, had got there first, although she was so slow in launching that Henry Blogg had decided to launch the Cromer boat.

That was the first of very many similar fruitless trips while Henry Blogg was coxswain. The men groused and swore, but knew that the fatigue and frustration of those trips had to be set against the satisfaction of taking a terrified, desperate man out of the rigging of his broken ship.

The first record of the name Henry Blogg is found in the Cromer branch minute book for the Annual Meeting, January 13, 1909:

> It was agreed that full authority be given to Henry Blogg to act as coxswain during the temporary disablement of J. Harrison.

'Buttons' Harrison was unable to carry on, so in November the crew got together to propose to the branch committee the man they wanted as coxswain. Most of them were afraid that a tee-totaller coxswain would mean the end of many jolly evenings in some bar parlour, when the lifeboat rewards were paid out. The names of Henry Blogg and George Rook were put forward – and Henry Blogg was the teetotaller! It was a close contest and possibly the men realised that something more than a jolly evening was at stake, for the teetotaller won by a single vote!

Then, on December 4, a committee meeting was held in the Red Lion Hotel and sixty fishermen were present as well as committee members, to give expression on three appointments. James Harrison's resignation through ill health was accepted and when the question of a successor came up Harry Balls proposed Henry Blogg as coxswain-superintendent. This was agreed to unanimously. The bright new star was climbing into a clear sky where many stars already shone and from that night it was to rise to be the brightest of them all.

The young coxswain got away to a good start, for, in addition to his background and his inherited love of the sea, he had great gifts of tenacity, daring and judgement. Moreover, John James had passed on to the young man the many lessons he had learned. Some men can give advice but not take it – Henry Blogg had the wisdom to take the advice so generously given to him.

Henry was then living in Swan Yard, Church Street and the understanding was that when the maroons went he would meet John James near the top of the gangway, now granite-paved. He got advice on tide and wind, what it would probably be like on the sands and what to do in such and such a case. It was good schooling and Henry knew it. He made mistakes and when he realised what he had done wrong he took care he did not make them again. One of his earliest mistakes nearly brought disaster and the end of his career. It was a case of his daring out-stripping his good sense – and Henry Blogg was not the first, and unlikely to be the last, young man guilty of that mistake!

Henry Blogg pictured in the sternsheets of the Louisa Heartwell *lifeboat.*

4

A Young Hand at the Helm

HENRY BLOGG'S first service as official coxswain was to the three-master barque *Alf*, although his election did not take place until a week later. He had, however, been given full authority to act as coxswain, ten months earlier, for James Harrison was too ill to take the helm.

The *Alf* was a fine rescue, hall-marked with the qualities that made Blogg famous. It was an appetiser for the good things to come and demonstrated that this beardless youth, this reticent, teetotal fisherman, was a leader of men.

The *Alf*, 1066 tons, of Laurug, went aground on the dreaded Haisborough Sands, on Tuesday, November 23, 1909. There were fifteen men on board and she had crossed the North Sea safely from Porsgrund, in Oslo Fjord, to Liverpool with a cargo of wood. It was night-time, foggy and very cold and although the anxious Norwegian skipper had kept an intent watch, he had failed to see the light-vessel through the clammy shroud and had ploughed into the sands three miles south-east of the lightship. The wind was strong and coming from the north-west by west; it set the fog eddying in swirling patches. A heavy sea was running on the sands which immediately began to pound its victim to death.

The captain saw that nothing he could do would get his ship free; you cannot order 'full speed astern' on a sailing-barque. He had been too long at sea not to know that the lifting and banging of his ship on the sands would strain her timbers and cause her to break up. He dreaded this Norfolk coast and these rapacious sands, which he knew had caused the death of hundreds of stout ships. He thought his best policy would be to launch the ship's boats and try to get clear of the sandbank, as the fog was so thick that flares were unlikely to be seen. He hoped that if they could get into quieter waters they might make the shore.

He gave orders to get the boats away. The first mate would take the port boat and he would take the starboard. His boat was successfully launched and the first mate was about to get into his boat with the second mate behind him when a wave caught it and flung it away from the ship, breaking all ropes and leaving the two men still on the wreck. There was no hope of the boat getting back alongside the barque and the two men had to watch, fearful and helpless, while the two boats with their thirteen comrades drifted away and were swallowed up by the darkness. The turmoil of torn sails lashing the mast and spars in frenzy added to the fury of the sea and the sense of desertion, in being left behind on a wreck that was already breaking up, must have been almost unbearable for those two men.

But, had they known it, things were faring even worse with the boats.

The carpenter took charge of the port boat and the men had pulled only a hundred yards when a wave caught and capsized it, flinging them into the icy sea. The other boat was close enough to see the disaster, though wisps of fog were blown around their light. They tried to get to the struggling men, but three of them were drowned before they reached the spot and hauled in the others.

There were now ten men in the starboard boat, which was so overloaded that every oncoming wave threatened to swamp it. So much water was shipped that, despite desperate and constant baling, the water gained on them. The captain encouraged his men to keep rowing and baling until somehow, by frantic endeavour, they got clear of the breakers on the sands and into deeper water where they had a better chance of keeping their little craft afloat.

There was small hope of being picked up in the dark and so their main aim was to keep afloat until daylight when they could try to reach the land. So, through the night, drenched by sea and

A photographic portrait of Henry Blogg, probably by London society photographer Olive Edis, who was based in Sheringham.

fog, numb and stiff with the bitter cold, they baled and baled to keep down the water and prayed for the dawn.

With the first light of dawn their spirits rose, for the fog had mostly gone, although ragged streamers still came in with the raw wind. One man fastened his drenched coat to an oar and hoisted it as a distress signal. Although only a tiny thing in that waste of wind-lashed waters, it worked. There was a hoarse wild cry of 'Look! Look! A ship! A ship!' from one of the men and the others stopped their rowing and baling to stare with red bleary eyes to where the stiff finger pointed and – indistinct as she was – in the haze there they saw the *Chanticleer* coming out of the dawn. They were then just a few miles from Cromer and their condition was pitiable. One of the seamen who had been thrown into the water when the port boat capsized was unconscious. He was taken on board the *Chanticleer* where they did everything they could to revive him, but he died from exposure on the way to Yarmouth, where the other nine survivors, more dead than alive, were landed.

Back on the *Alf*, the two marooned men watched the sea remorselessly destroying their ship. Their position seemed hopeless and death only a short time away unless help was brought quickly to them. They found some flares in the ship's stores and lit them at irregular intervals, watching the vivid light illuminate the confused sea and swirling mist.

Their signals were seen – not from the shore but by the Haisbro' light-vessel. The master, twelve miles out at sea, immediately telephoned the coastguard. It was 10.15 p.m. when the message reached Cromer. The secretary and new coxswain were consulted and the maroons boomed dully in the fog. By 11 p.m. the *Louisa Heartwell* was entering the surf with seventeen men on board and forty drenched launchers silhouetted in the eerie light of paraffin flares.

Henry Blogg had received a few hasty but precious words of advice from his stepfather and soon after launching he hoisted the lugsail and hurried as best he could through the storm and darkness to the distant sands. The advice had been to get more information from the light vessel about the position of the flares and by 1 a.m. young Henry Blogg was hailing its master. He gave the lifeboat an accurate bearing and said he had seen more flares an hour earlier. The lifeboat turned south.

Twenty minutes later, the bowman discerned the dark shape of a masted ship and they drew nearer, burning white hand-lights. Once alongside the wreck, they shouted and called. They could see the boats were gone, but there was no sign of life. Only the crash of heavy seas, the wailing of the wind in the rigging and the flapping of torn canvas answered their calls. The fog drifted over them into the surrounding darkness. The ship was abandoned – they were too late. The only thing to do was to search for the ship's boats in case they needed help.

So the fourteen oarsmen of the *Louisa Heartwell* pulled away from the *Alf* and began beating around in the clammy darkness of the early morning. Every man peered about him into the mist and night, but the chances of finding the boats in that sea were pitifully remote.

After several hours of vain searching, Henry Blogg decided it was time to return home; but they had fifteen miles to go with both wind and tide against them. The crew were exhausted after hours of rowing in that heavy sea, so the young coxswain decided to make a landfall at Palling and anchor until the tide was more favourable and his men had rested.

They reached Palling and lay at anchor two hours. The grey dawn broke over the grey sea and the fog thinned as the daylight strengthened. Henry Blogg thought it was time to go home. He was about to give the order to weigh anchor when, suddenly, he saw the smoke of a vessel as it emerged from the haze. Slowly, the ship came towards them. Blogg watched for several minutes, then he heard the shriek of her whistle, repeated again and again. It was a steam drifter with obviously something urgent to say, so he weighed anchor from the lee of the land and went out to the ship. The message was urgent and surprising. At dawn the drifter *King* had seen a wreck on the sands and, going as close as she dared in the early light, had distinguished two men clinging to the mizzen rigging!

Henry Blogg blamed himself for not making absolutely sure that the wreck had been abandoned. They had searched the sea around for half the night, while all the time those two men were clinging to their ship. Blogg was, nevertheless, puzzled by their failure to answer his calls. At the time the lifeboat had been alongside and her crew had hailed, both men were below looking for paraffin and materials to make improvised flares. The noise of the waves and the flapping of cordage and ragged canvas had drowned the shouts of the lifeboat-men.

With all speed, Blogg put back for the sands, his crew bending and pulling in an all-out effort to get to the wreck without further delay, each man hoping that they would still be in time. In his mind's eye Henry Blogg could see the two half-frozen men lashed to the rigging while the sea broke against their vessel, reaching up in an endeavour to break their precarious hold. His blue eyes were fixed and the young face wet with spray was tense as Henry Blogg saw the seas breaking, white and angry, on the sand. Then, through the mist, he distinguished the barque and when he saw the two small dark shapes in the rigging he knew there was still a chance.

As the lifeboat got closer the crew saw that the *Alf* had broken in two and that her cargo of timber was being washed out of her. Big waves were running right over the battered hulk and flinging cascades of salt water over the men near the mast.

It was rough on the sands, even for a lifeboat, but they had to act promptly – the men must be so exhausted and numb that they would never secure a line.

There is no operation in seamanship more difficult than to bring a boat alongside a vessel in a heavy breaking sea, but Henry Blogg brought the boat under the lee quarter of the wreck and bowman Jack Davies got a grapnel on to the *Alf*. A heavy sea struck the *Louisa Heartwell* severely on the stern and for a moment it seemed she would be swept away, but she swung back and held her position. Two oars were snapped like matchsticks by that sea. The two Norwegians, seeing help so near, found the willpower and strength to move their half-frozen, almost rigid, bodies down the rigging and over the sea-washed deck to the lifeboat. Eager hands dragged them on board. They were so exhausted, they just lay as they fell until the lifeboat-men, whose oars had snapped, began attending to them.

It was only with great difficulty that the lifeboat got away from the dead ship and off the sands. The seas ran at her from three directions and four more oars were broken before they finally struggled into deep water.

With six oars gone and a contrary wind, there was no hope of reaching Cromer. The men they had saved were in such a serious condition that the quickest and wisest course was to hoist sail and make for Yarmouth. When they landed the two mates of the *Alf*, the lifeboat-men had been at sea for fifteen hours.

It had been a stern struggle, but through good teamwork this difficult rescue had been effected. Henry Blogg was the first to admit that one man does not make a team. He knew, as a keen football fan, that, however good the captain may be, he can win no matches without the help of his team. Henry Blogg was the first to give credit to his 'team'. Nothing pleased him more than to hear his men praised or to see them decorated. In later years, when returning from some great service, he would say a few words of praise about his crew and let it go at that – there was no word of his personal achievement.

The team that 'played' for Cromer which Henry Blogg captained for thirty-eight years was one of the finest in the lifeboat service. They trusted each other implicitly and where Blogg led they would go. He inspired them. Brave and selfless as they were they took from him the light of higher courage and a readiness to go beyond normal endeavour and endurance. The test of great leadership is not in getting men to do what is expected of them, but in doing what seems impossible. Henry Blogg had that power over men. They trusted him, not with just the share of a salvage job, but with their lives. If a voice was raised saying an enterprise was too risky, or Blogg had attempted too much, they would say, 'Henry knows what he's a'doin'.' And he did. The service to the *Alf* had proved his right to lead. His men knew he would risk more and endure more than he asked of them. Once at sea, his was the decisive voice and the responsibility. He was prepared to make big decisions and account for them. Only once did he give way to the clamour for a course against his own judgement – and that nearly brought utter disaster.

There was a lot of talk about the service to the *Alf* and people outside Cromer took notice that there was a capable young coxswain at this station. Capable in seamanship and possessing that not-so-common quality – common sense. In Norfolk dialect Henry Blogg 'wus no fule'. He had a good head on his shoulders and a memory that his nephew Henry Davies likened to a tape-recording machine. For faces, facts and names it was surprisingly retentive. It happened many times in the beach business that a visitor hired a hut and then did not come again to Cromer for four or five years. But, on going to the attendant with the cloth cap on his head and the galaxy of medals in a box at home, he might say, 'Do you remember me, Mr Blogg?' and the wrinkled face would form more wrinkles and then Henry Blogg would say, 'Yes, you were here five seasons ago. You are Mr So-and-so. I think you had hut Number Six!'

A strong constitution partnered that strong character and was well treated! He was a temperate man and when the sea and the service of humanity demanded more endurance and stamina than a man should be expected to give, he was able to find and give it. He bore unflinchingly the intense strain of the War years, the physical and mental stress of services lasting many days and nights; sleepless, hungry and wet through for days on end, he carried on.

He had few illnesses in his life. He was ruptured while hauling in crab-pots; he had appendicitis and was operated upon at the age of sixty-two. But for all his exposure through hundreds of launches, he kept remarkably free from colds and rheumatism. His flesh was quick to heal. If he did get a knock he went to the iodine bottle and bandaged up the wound. He was a firm believer in friar's balsam, both internally and externally. Most fishermen suffer from poisoned hands through handling hooks and bait, but not Henry Blogg.

He tried to give hospitals, doctors and dentists the widest possible berth, although when he did go to the two former he had the best of treatment. He had no dealings with dentists and endured toothache until he could himself pull out the weakened molar. When he lost all his teeth he would not have artificial ones but let his gums take on the extra work.

Henry Blogg was a believer in the usual superstitions of the fishermen – anything loaded into the boat, such as nets or pots, had to go in over the starboard gunwale. He always tried to go to his boats the same way and if he had to go round by another street and things went wrong that day, he would blame the break in routine. He did not like the number 13, or starting an enterprise on a Friday. When taking out the floorboards of his boat they had to be put on one side the same way up as in the boat; they must not be turned over! But when adversity hit him he was heard to say about luck, 'Whatever you do it doesn't make any difference. There's only one sort of luck and that's bad.'

In his weather-assessment he coupled science with lore. He would consult his barometer before going to sea and in later years always tried to hear the weather forecast but he was not bound by what the meteorological experts predicted. He had been brought up to observe the sky and sea for portents of weather and he knew them to be reliable. He could 'feel' a change in the weather without looking at the 'glass'. He would say:

> Evening grey and morning red
> Makes a fisherman shake his head.
> Evening red and morning grey
> Is the sure sign of a very fine day.

Or 'The gulls are playing "gatter"', which meant approaching rough weather. `The water's turned sheer (clear)' was the sign to him of an approaching onshore wind.

He read a green-coloured sky or a 'mackerel' sky and also 'double-headed' clouds, as signs of wind. A 'shepherd's-flock' sky – patches of white cloud like a flock of sheep – meant rain within twenty-four hours.

It was only a month after the excellent service to the *Alf* that the Cromer boat put up another fine show. In fact, when asked what rescues stood out in his mind, the first one Jack Davies mentioned was to the barquentine *Albatross*. He rubbed his thigh as the blazing fire made it tingle while he recalled the bitter cold of that December morning in 1909. 'There were black men on that wreck,' Davies said. 'Poor devils! We saved some of them, but they were so stiff with cold they could not sit down.'

The *Albatross* of Lowestoft was a 340-ton three-master carrying coal from Hartlepool to Yarmouth.

'She was one of the smartest sailing-colliers round the coast,' said her captain proudly.

Like the *Alf*, she ran on to the Haisborough Sands, in a thick haze and at the same spot, and it is said that she actually struck the submerged wreck. She was making a spanking pace when she ran into the sands and the jolt that brought down her masts in a crashing, splintering tangle flung the crew of eight in all directions.

It was 2.45 a.m. when the Bacton coastguard reported to Cromer that the light-vessel had seen flares in the direction of the sands and at 3.20 a.m., in the freezing cold and darkness, the *Louisa Heartwell* was launched.

It takes the highest form of courage to answer the summons of the maroons at 3 a.m. on a bitter December morning. There is no stirring roll of drums or bugle-call, no flags flying, no encouraging roar of spectators – only the cold, the roaring sea and the all-enveloping darkness.

The secretary recorded in his report:

> The response to the rocket-signals was one of the smartest on record. The rapidity with which the crew mustered and got away was a surprise to not a few who, being awakened by the signal, had turned out to see the launch. By the time they were on the beach the lifeboat was going down the slipway and was very soon getting clear of the breakers.

Henry Blogg remembered the *Albatross* better than anyone,

for it was not only one of his first rescues as coxswain, but it might well have been his last! It taught him that however great the need, however daring a man may be, there are some things he must not do. On this service he ignored the counsel given him by the Palling lifeboatmen – 'Never go on the sands in the dark, when you can't see what you're doing. Moonlight? Yes. But never in the dark.'

The *Louisa Heartwell* made for the light-vessel to learn the position of the flares and at 6 a.m. she was near enough to the *Albatross* to hear the cries of the wrecked men. Wreckage was floating all around; masts were gone; big seas were sweeping the decks.

In the darkness they had great difficulty in getting alongside and one sea, catching Henry Blogg by surprise, swept the lifeboat under the overhanging stern of the *Albatross*, so that she could not ride and would have been held down while the next sea went over her. The oarsmen shoved frantically at the slippery stern of the ship and just as a great breaker came rolling towards them – and it seemed that they must be overwhelmed – they moved the *Louisa Heartwell* slightly away, so that the wave washed her almost clear. The lifeboat struck her gunwale on the ship, but that was slight damage compared with what might have happened. Had that sea struck her squarely there would have been a major disaster.

Once more they brought the lifeboat round and this time bowman Jack Davies successfully hooked a grapnel in the deck. The crew of the barquentine was taken off as their ship was torn to pieces.

The drenched, bedraggled captain of the *Albatross*, stammering uncontrollably through chattering teeth, told Henry Blogg that a crew member, Frank Gale, was adrift in a small boat. He had started to bale out the ship's small boat and had been caught by a big sea, which snapped the painter, setting the boat adrift. The despair and dread of that man must have exceeded that of the two mates stranded on the *Alf*. The captain feared the boat had capsized, as it was waterlogged when it broke adrift.

While his crew attended to the rescued men, half-dead with

Henry Blogg at home at Swallow Cottage.

cold and with clothes frozen on them, Henry Blogg's mind turned ever to that man adrift in those wicked seas. The lifeboat-men took off their own warm stockings and coats to put on the rescued men who were suffering intensely and as Henry Blogg watched them he knew he must get them to shelter without delay. Yet it seemed wrong to leave the sands without looking for that little boat. The young coxswain was in a dilemma. It was a grave responsibility – to save a life and possibly lose lives. It would be light in another hour and he could search the sands more quickly, but that hour might mean death to one of the rescued men.

Meanwhile, both the Winterton and Palling lifeboats had been launched and had reached the sands. Knowing the danger better than Henry Blogg, they were standing by in deep water waiting for daylight. When Henry Blogg was coming from the wreck, keeping a sharp lookout for the little boat, he saw the outline of the Winterton lifeboat and burned a handlight to attract attention. When they came up he told them he had got the crew of the *Albatross* but one man was adrift and he asked them to continue the search while he hurried the suffering survivors to shelter.

As with the service to the *Alf*, both wind- and tide-stream made a return to Cromer impossible, so once again they made for Yarmouth. The *Onyx*, an Ipswich steamer, seeing them, gave them a welcome tow to the harbour mouth and the rescued men were quickly got to the Mariners' Refuge while the *Louisa Heartwell* put into a shipyard for temporary repairs.

For all Henry Blogg's error in going on to the sands in the dark, he had again demonstrated his sound judgement and seamanship. 'Young "Ry" knows what he's doing' was the crew's reiterated verdict. 'Ry' was Henry Blogg's nickname, although rarely used to his face.

There was a lot of excitement on the beach on April 20, 1910. The signal called the crew to help the Norwegian ship *Haakon* – and nearly all of them were crab fishing.

The boats were quietly pursuing their task when the maroons cracked. There was a stir like a sudden squall, or a crust thrown to the gulls, among the crabbing-fleet. Boat after boat in full sail came scurrying to the shore. The men just tumbled out of their boats and rushed up the beach to get their lifeboat gear while friends hauled up their fishing boats. It was a moving testimony to the priority of the lifeboat, for the fisherman vows that, whatever happens to his fishing, the lifeboat must go out. And the result? When they reached the sands they found the Palling boat had completed the rescue. They might have kept on with their crabbing!

In the years before the First World War there were a surprisingly large number of such fruitless calls, particularly in 1911 when time after time the lifeboat reached the distant Haisborough Sands and found no further trace of a vessel. Or, as on May 1 that year, when the Palling, Winterton, Gorleston and Caister lifeboats, as well as the *Louisa Heartwell*, went to the sands only to find the vessel had refloated and got away.

But it was better to answer a dozen unprofitable calls than miss saving one life. The Cromer boat did save many lives in those years, including twenty-one from the Belgian fishing-boat, *St Antoine de Padoue*, in addition to many Norfolk fishermen who got into difficulties.

A typical Blogg touch was to persuade the crew to improve the already fine boat, *Louisa Heartwell*, by getting a taller mast and another suit of sails. It made her one of the fastest and best of all row-and-sail lifeboats. She covered the twelve miles to the sands in less than an hour on more than one occasion and her best time was probably better than that of a motorboat. The crew, of course, had to pay for the change themselves and there were a few grumbles, but the coxswain knew how to handle men; with a word of praise here and a little banter there he got what he wanted.

Henry Blogg had a quiet sense of humour and he sometimes squeezed a joke out of very grim situations. His laugh was almost noiseless and began with a shaking of the body; as though he was trying to keep it all inside himself.

He loved a Norfolk yarn and when he saw Jimmy Dumble, coxswain of the Sheringham boat, steering a course for him across the beach, he knew he was going to get one. At one time there was a feud between Cromer and Sheringham (Cromer Crabs versus the Shannocks) and it was unsafe for a Cromer fisherman to show himself in the other town, or a Sheringham man to appear in Cromer. The Queensberry rules were laid aside and stones and sticks were freely used. Many a man carried ugly scars to prove that the brotherhood of the sea ended on the land – at least, this corner of it. But gradually the bitterness lessened and only flared up when Cromer and Sheringham met on the football ground, when anything could happen. Jimmy Dumble and

The lifeboat Louisa Heartwell *with the extra sail Henry Blogg fitted to an oar, in an effort to gain a little extra help from a favourable wind.*

Henry Blogg could meet without wondering if the other carried a knuckle-duster and Jimmy's tales would be retold to the Cromer crew, losing something in dialect, for Henry's dialect was not strong.

The tale that Henry Blogg got from Jimmy and retailed for years concerned a farm worker who kept a dog but never paid a licence. Everything was all right while the old 'bobby' was there, but when he retired the new constable had more zeal for his duty and sympathy for the Inland Revenue.

Walking down the street with his dog one day, the man suddenly saw the new policeman turn a corner and come towards him. He quickly propelled the dog into a yard with his boot and continued down the street. But the policeman stopped him.

'What about that dog of yours?'

'Hint got no dawg.'

'Oh, where is it, then?'

'Tha's dead.'

'Dead! When did it die?'

'Let's see, if thet owd dawg h'd lived ter next Tuesday, he'd 'a bin dead a fortnight,' said the man passing on, leaving the constable to work that one out.

He would also couple that story with the tale of the two holidaymakers who fancied some cockles and asked a local fisherman if he could help them. He said he could, so that evening they took him in their car to a coastal village and while one visitor sat in the vehicle beside the road the other accompanied the fisherman to a house near the beach. It was deep dusk. They went to the door, the fisherman tried the handle and opening the door he bawled, 'A-g-g-i-e . . . are yer there, A-g-g-i-e. . . . ?'

There was no answer. The house was dark and still. So they went round to the back. There the old man opened a window, muttering to himself all the time and, putting his head into the dark room, called out in a voice that was heard by the other visitor on the road, 'A-g-g-i-e . . . here's Mister Blyth arter some cockles.'

The holidaymaker was embarrassed and walked away. He heard his friend call again and then the door opened, followed by the sound of subdued voices. Presently the old fisherman joined him and explained apologetically, 'I carn't git yer no cockles ternight, cors they int verra bright in theer. Poor owd Aggie's lyin' in her box in thet room where I hollered!'

An incident typical of Henry Blogg occurred one day when the coxswain was talking to his solicitor, Henry Murrell, at his beach hut; a pompous young man with a supercharged 'Oxford' accent strode up and broke in upon the conversation by asking, 'Where will I find Captain Blogg?'

Henry Blogg bristled immediately; he did not like the approach and he did not like his title.

'I don't know,' he said very slowly.

'Don't know? Surely you know where he is? Isn't he here?'

'I don't know.'

'But I was told I should find him here. I want to meet him.'

Henry Blogg's face was expressionless – 'I'm afraid I can't help you.'

The young man put several more sharp questions, the colour mounting in his cheeks, but he got no further. Finally, he turned on his heel in a huff and walked away.

Before he was out of sight Blogg's eyes were twinkling and he was shaking with noiseless laughter. He turned to Henry Murrell. 'I didn't tell him a lie, did I, Murrell? I didn't tell him a lie – I'm not a captain, am I?'

Many other visitors to Cromer passed the thickset person in the cloth cap and blue gansey standing looking at the sea, without realising that the homely figure was one of the most famous seamen in a county of seamen – and, indeed, of a seafaring country.

Most of us find it hard to visualise a hero in the plain workaday garb of the sea. We want to dress him in serge with gold braid and glittering medals. But Henry Blogg was no film star of romance. He was a fisherman, working in coarse garments, often smelling of fish and tar, earning his living by toiling on the sea and offering his skill and energy to man the local lifeboat when need arose. And if he was not dashingly handsome there was dignity in his face and bearing. He had the medals all right – in a drawer at home. And if his friends wanted to see them they had to wait until he was out and ask his wife to show them!

So perhaps it was not to be wondered at that many a visitor who had read of his exploits chatted with him and went away without knowing that the civil fisherman with the very blue eyes, narrowed and circled with wrinkles from a lifetime of looking across the sea, was the great Henry Blogg. Yes, 'great' is the word, for although in many ways he was typical of the East Anglian longshore fishermen he was not an ordinary fisherman – he was unique. His record of life saving was unequalled in the history of the lifeboat service. He won the Institution's Gold Medal three times and its Silver Medal four times; the Empire Gallantry Medal in 1924, which was replaced by the George Cross (instituted in 1940); the British Empire Medal in 1941; the Queen's Coronation Medal; an Italian medal and one from the Canine Defence Society.

5

The First World War

THE FIRST World War brought its own problems and opportunities. Cromer soon lost some of its younger members for war service, so that the lifeboat had to be manned by the older men. Moreover, as early as 1915, life at night was made unpleasant by Zeppelins, which chose Cromer as their entrance from the North Sea. It was not the damage they did, but night after night the drone of their engines coming in and going out made sleep impossible. Then came the searchlights to stab the night and pick out the cigar-shaped intruders. Although Henry Blogg took little notice, his wife and daughter dreaded them.

Henry Blogg had plenty to occupy mind and body, for, although the beach business was much diminished, fishing was accompanied by many new risks and the lifeboat was in greater demand. The *New Oporto* of West Hartlepool was one of many calls that kept him busy. This 260-ton vessel, with a cargo mostly of iron, went aground very close to, if not on the actual spot, where both the *Alf* and *Albatross* had stranded on the Haisborough Sands. It was January 8, 1915 and, although there was a strong breeze, the sea was only moderate.

The Palling lifeboat arrived first and a council of war was held aboard the *New Oporto* as the master thought he might save his ship by jettisoning the cargo. Cromer put seven lifeboatmen aboard and Palling also put men aboard and they began throwing the iron

Launching the Louisa Heartwell, *probably for a Lifeboat Day. The young Henry Blogg is amongst the crew whilst cox'n Jimmy 'Buttons' Harrison takes the helm.*

into the sea. They worked steadily from 10 a.m. until nearly 8 p.m. Then the sea grew rougher and the tide raced like water through a sluice. The hatches had to be closed. Three hours later they found a couple of feet of sinister black water in the stoke-hole and the ship began to heel slowly over. There was nothing for it but to abandon ship. The Palling boat went alongside and took off ten men and the Cromer seven and both made for home, leaving the *New Oporto* to be pounded to death by the sea. She became a total wreck in a matter of a few hours.

One of the worst nights during that war came ten days later when the boat was launched through a very heavy surf and the beach was an inch deep in hail. They managed to rescue both the crew and the ketch *Thomas Stratton*, but the *George Royle*, with all on board, perished on that wild night on Sheringham Shoal – not far from where the lifeboat had stood by the *Thomas Stratton* all night. They also saved fourteen men from the SS *Bodil* of Esjberg, after it had grounded on the sands. That was on May 27, 1916. The entire crew abandoned the doomed vessel and took to the ship's boat. They would have been swamped, had they not had the good sense to take oil in the boat and by pouring this on the water managed to survive until Henry Blogg, who was crossing the sands very cautiously – for it was low tide – spotted something sticking out of the sea in the distance. It was the boat, with an oar held upright to attract their attention.

That was a fortunate meeting and happy ending, but all stories did not end like that and although the life of Henry Blogg is bound up with some of the most magnificent rescues ever recorded, it is also linked with some of the grimmest tragedies of the sea.

It is not always the greatest loss of life or the wreck of the largest ship that touches our hearts the most – it is often only in the light of details that we can picture the scene and pale at the terror of shipwreck. Many a tragic wreck off the Norfolk coast can never be told, for time and again when the lifeboat reached the Haisborough Sands they found only the pathetic flotsam of a lost ship. Not one man had been spared from the foaming jaws to tell of the grinding jolt in the darkness, the hopes, the heroism, the sacrifice, the terror and despair as one by one the sea claimed its victims.

On Wednesday, January 12, 1916, the 860-ton SS *Havfru*, of Christiana, was struggling through filthy weather round the coast of Norfolk on her way to Amsterdam from Goole. Carrying a cargo of coal, she had left Hull at 8 o'clock that morning and the weather had worsened every mile and when darkness came the cosmopolitan crew of fourteen, including Russians, Dutchmen, Swedes, Danes and a Spaniard, were very apprehensive as they neared this dangerous coast. Their fears were well founded and in spite of their watchfulness the *Havfru* drove with shattering force on to the sands. It was then nearly 10 p.m. By this time the raging gale made escape impossible; the Haisborough Sands would never let them go. The crew therefore tried to launch a small boat and three seamen got into it, but the waves picked up the boat like a nutshell and dashed it against the vessel. The three men were flung into the water. Two of them grabbed ropes which were flung to them, but the third was washed away.

There seemed now no hope of getting away from the doomed ship and as the great waves smashed upon their vessel every seaman wondered just how long she could last. The merciless breakers caught three or four more men and dragged them off the ship. Two were clinging to rails, but the weight of water tore them away. The rest of the crew climbed into the rigging and clung there hoping that by some miracle they had been seen from the shore and help might reach them.

On the Thursday morning the second engineer – a big, burly man – decided he might as well die making a bid for his life as hang in the rigging suffering agonies and finally drop into the sea from exposure. A small boat remained on the ship. Having made his choice, the engineer managed to reach it and, choosing his moment, cut the mooring rope and got away. They saw the big form pulling madly at the oars, then he was lost to sight in spray and yeasty foam. He was never seen again. His chances of surviving in those seas were made even smaller, for apparently the boat was waterlogged when it got away.

While this grim drama was being enacted on the sands the life-saving organisation of Norfolk was already active. Lifeboat-men on the lookout off Palling had seen a lighted ship drive on to the sands. They immediately tried to launch their boat, but the tide was very high and the seas so heavy that despite all their efforts they could not get away.

A telephone message was put through to Cromer telling them of their struggles and failure to launch. The spring was touched off at Cromer and the men of the *Louisa Heartwell* tried to do what Palling could not; but the exceptional tide and heavy seas beat them. Henry Blogg and his men stood by throughout the rest of that night and the whole of January 13. They talked, played cards, ate, drank, fretted and waited. It was a rare thing for Cromer men to be beaten in launching, but they were helpless in that sea. They hoped the weather would improve and enable them to get out to the sands, but when night came down the wind and seas grew worse. Great waves thundered against the sea walls and cascaded like bursting shells over the promenade and came foaming and swirling into the boathouse itself.

Henry Blogg and the secretary talked it over. There was still nothing to be done but wait for the dawn and hope the seas would moderate. So for another long spell they waited while the gale beat with full fury upon the coast. Henry Blogg paced up and down in frustration, his mind on the ship they could not aid and the seamen possibly even then clinging for life to deck or rigging.

When the day did break there was a definite improvement and as it was hoped that, after all those hours during which they had been helpless, someone might yet have possibly survived, they decided to launch.

Even with the improvement in the weather the launch was difficult. The sea with the tide behind it was very high, although not so high as on the 13th. Great heaving masses broke in a riot of churned water, so that the launchers led by Tom 'Bussey' Allen had to wade waist-deep into the icy sea to complete the launch, but by 8.25 a.m. the crew were pulling clear of the broken water.

Henry Blogg set a straight course for the Haisbro' light-vessel to get more detailed information. But the master of the vessel could not help. He knew nothing of the wreck and had seen no distress signals. This meant a search. For nearly two hours the lifeboat beat around the edge of the Middle Haisbro' looking in vain for the wreck. They were too late, or the Palling men were mistaken and it was all a wild goose chase! Then someone with keen sight saw a mast sticking out above the waters. That was all! The ship and the crew had perished in that awful storm while the would-be rescuers had been forced to play cards. Suddenly

Jack Davies, standing in the bows, yelled, 'There's a man on that mast!'

Every man stared as the boat drew nearer and they all saw the dark sagging shape hanging at the mast. When they got closer to the vessel they saw one half was completely under the water and the other half all except one mast. Henry Blogg manoeuvred the *Louisa Heartwell* with great care and brilliant seamanship until he was as near as he dared get and the man, who had seemed to revive at their shouts and the thought of being saved, tried to loose the ropes that held him. His arms moved a little, then he sagged sideways. A few minutes passed and he rallied and some- how his stiff fingers worked and he managed to get some of the way down the rigging unaided. When lifted into the lifeboat he again collapsed. He had been thirty-six hours in that rigging in the most terrible conditions of exposure and cold. His hands and feet were horribly swollen and chafed raw through being lashed for so long to the mast. Salt had crystallised in his hair and on his face. 'My God! What he has suffered!' muttered an old lifeboat- man, as he tried to force rum between his teeth.

The sole survivor of the *Havfru* was twenty-three-year old Niels Nielson, a Dane from Copenhagen. He had been the don- keyman on the ship.

It was learned later that after the burly second engineer had got away from the wreck Captain Berg, the chief mate, three sailors and Nielson had been left. Then, in the early afternoon of January 14, a savage sea had hit the stranded ship and with a rending crash had broken it in two. It also clawed from the rigging four men, including the captain, leaving Nielson and a sailor. They saw their struggling, crying comrades carried away by that great roaring sea, the sound of their last fearful screams had risen above the storm and filled the hearts of the survivors with horror.

The two men climbed higher into the rigging of the mainmast lest a similar sea snatch them also. There for hour after hour they suffered intense pain from exposure. Sometimes praying, sometimes weeping, trying to move their stiffening limbs and crying out in fresh agony of movement. Occasionally, a big wave reached up at them and spray and spindrift continually flew over them.

At first they tried to cheer each other with an occasional shout, but that seemed a mockery and they soon got past shouting. As the night wore on in hour after hour of agony and terror hope died and death assumed a fair guise, for it would end their suffering. When the grey fingers of dawn stretched across the sea Nielson saw his companion was more dead than alive, yet he still hung on while below the merciless sea crashed and swirled over the decks of their ship.

At 9 o'clock, after surviving over thirty hours in the stays of the mainmast, the sailor just dropped off into the waiting sea. No wave had snatched at him. He had just reached the limit of suffering and endurance. Nielson, left alone, did not know how he found the strength of body and will to hang on after this man dropped into the water. What he endured during that eternity of torment seemed to have burned away all feeling and dullness and numbness took the edge off agony. He was dimly aware that the lifeboat was approaching, but felt no joy or relief. It did not matter to him. He was past further suffering or caring. He remembered feeling surprised that he was able to release himself from the rigging and wondered who were the bearded men in sou'westers bending over him.

The lifeboat-men rubbed and chafed the swollen, bleeding limbs of the rescued man, trying to restore circulation in the stone-like body while the other oarsmen pulled away from these pitiless, murderous sands. Deep in the heart of fishermen there is a true love of the sea, but the sight of the young Dane made them curse its brutality.

It was a terrific pull home against the wind. The oilskin-clad crew strained at the oars in grim silence as they struggled against the oncoming seas. Fortunately a collier, seeing their ordeal, came to their assistance and towed them almost home. The oarsmen shipped their oars, straightened their aching backs and blessed the inventor of steam-power.

The *Louisa Heartwell* had shipped a lot of water and had become almost unmanageable. It was with great difficulty, after they slipped the tow, that Henry Blogg beached her. Nielson was lifted ashore and rushed to the hospital where he was promptly treated. Such was his amazing constitution that not many hours later he was able to talk to a reporter while some soldiers who were in the same ward listened spellbound to his terrible story.

The magnificent service to the *Fernebo* in January 1917 had stirred the public imagination and had put the name of Henry Blogg on thousands of lips. Even in time of war, when great deeds were being performed on land and sea, Norfolk people still talked of that great rescue on the sea front.

Henry Blogg did not help to keep the talk going for he was an uncommunicative man. Although on good terms with local journalists, Henry Blogg mistrusted strange pressmen, for he complained that when he told them one thing they reported another. When a reporter urged him for dramatic details to build up a highly coloured story from his plain unvarnished tale, he would draw right into his shell. Without wishing to be rude – for his kindly nature made him averse to hurting anyone by deed or word – his answers would grow shorter and farther apart until the questioner decided that, in addition to crabs and lobsters, there were oysters at Cromer.

He was most careful about passing an opinion of other lifeboat rescues or mishaps until he had read the RNLI journal containing the authentic account – and then he usually kept his opinion to himself.

In fact, it was difficult to get his opinion on many subjects. In his reading Henry would first absorb any news connected with lifeboats, then he would study political developments, for he was a keen follower of party politics at a national level. Alec Jackson was his friend for twenty-eight years before he knew which political party he favoured! The man who wanted to draw him into a political argument would be disappointed, for he would not be drawn. He knew not only how to keep a secret but – what is harder – how to keep an opinion. Many a man who has wrecked a friendship on the rocks of political or religious argument would do well to take a leaf out of this fisherman's book. Henry Blogg never had an enemy in the world, but he had his critics, for no man can go through seventy-eight years of mixing with other human beings without encountering criticism. But he was never criticised for what he said because he did not say it.

There was a humorous side to this reticence. On one occasion an official of the RNLI came from London to get an additional report from him on a spectacular service. Henry Blogg disappeared for most of the day, but in the end, when he was cornered, the District Inspector said, 'Look here, Blogg, Mr X has come all the way from London specially to see you.'

'Well, sir,' replied the coxswain, 'Here I am. He can see me,' and hurried off without another word.

He never gave his wife many details of his rescues – which must have been trying, to say the least, when Ann was so intensely proud of him. After a service he would often return home, change, have a meal and then relax in his favourite armchair. His wife had probably plied him with questions and received the typically manlike answer, 'Oh, you wouldn't understand about that.' When, later, a reporter sought an account of the service, Henry Blogg would be lying with his head well back and eyes almost closed, his hands cupped behind his head. His wife would announce that Mr So-and-so from the `Believe-it-or-not Gazette' was seeking an account of the service. The coxswain would not move, but after a long pause and much questioning, would say, 'Well, you'd better ask my wife. She knows all about that.'

There was a streak of impish humour in Henry Blogg.

An Institution official was once accompanying the crew on a practice launch. He was standing on the lifeboat deck as she slid down the slipway and only ducked at the very last moment to avoid hitting his head on the door lintel. Henry Blogg turned, grinning, to the crew and cried, 'There, we nearly took Mr X's head off.'

Later, as the boat was returning, the coxswain swung the boat off course, so that one of the crew could try to spear a shark with a boat hook.

'It was all delightfully informal and showed me that Henry Blogg could relax when he liked,' said the official. Samuel Johnson once said: 'Every man has a lurking wish to appear considerable in his native place.' Blogg did not dislike praise, especially when it included his crew and his own town, but he never sought it and his reports were noted for their understatements. Vice-Admiral Sir John Cunningham KCB said during the war, 'It was my duty a few weeks ago to read the minutes of an official inquiry into some work in which the Cromer lifeboat participated. If you had read the evidence of coxswain Blogg you would have thought that he had crossed the road to take the milk out of a baby's bottle.'

He never claimed more than was due. The waves were never bigger than he had to surmount nor the wind stronger than he had to face. In fact, few men have accomplished so much and said so little of their achievement.

The Cromer coxswain loved children and derived great joy from his daughter Queenie and from his many nieces and nephews. He liked having them with him at his beach hut and kept his eye on baby and pram many a time while mother got on with something else. It was a characteristic of his that the children he liked most he teased most. Sometimes he made them cry with vexation. Even gentle hair pulling was not barred. He would keep a ball that came his way, making the youngsters plead and plead for its return. But, of course, that little game was not always one-sided and Henry Blogg often missed things and had to 'plead' for their return! Henry Davies recalls how Uncle Henry once hung him on some railings at the top of the east wall so that he dangled, screaming and kicking, in space. Uncle had, of course, got one hand where he could have caught the youngster had his coat given way, but a female relative saw the little episode and gave Uncle Henry a piece of her mind for his idea of fun. That only pleased him the more!

He never forgot their birthdays, although he might overrun

the date. And he would hand his present to the child in person – never to the parent. Children sense child lovers and know when they are liked. In many family albums throughout the country there must be scores of snaps with the background of Cromer beach and in the foreground the world-famous coxswain and some youngsters with whom he had struck up a holiday acquaintance near his hut.

Henry and friends.

Outside the family one of his closest friends was a Dutchman, Martin van der Hidde, salvage officer on a Dutch tug based on Yarmouth. Henry Blogg saved him from the *Monte Nevoso* in 1932 and for the next six years they occasionally met on some service and were – as the Dutchman said – 'hailing welcome words across the water around the Haisborough Sands'. Later Martin van der Hidde paid many visits to Swallow Cottage, 'for,' he said, 'although we never talked very much, I know that he was always pleased to see me because I was one of the few out of more than eight hundred and seventy-three people he landed safely ashore who bothered to look him up or send a letter at Christmas.'

Henry Blogg was a man whom everybody had heard of and nobody really knew. Those who were nearest to him confess how small was their knowledge of his character. Although he was always meeting and mixing with people, he remained a solitary man, more shy than most people realised. He would plan with zest a surprise gift for a friend but become as embarrassed as a schoolgirl when giving it. As the Dutchman found, conversation came hard to him. When friends called at Swallow Cottage there would be breaks of ten minutes in the conversation during which he sat back in his chair staring at the fire, showing in a dozen ways his pleasure at the call but literally incapable of sustaining a flow of talk. His distaste for being fussed over and publicised was not assumed, it was genuine.

If Henry Blogg was a family man he was not a handyman! He might 'knock up' a coal-shed of sorts, but he could not fix a tap or a door-lock and he would not 'meddle with electricity' or motors. He began going to sea in the days of oar and sail and, although he moved with the times in most ways, he would have nothing to do with the motors of his own crab-boats. He left it to others to remedy any troubles. In fact, so scanty was his mechanical knowledge that in the early days of crab-boat engines he struck a match to see if there was any petrol in the tank. There was – and the tank blew up. Fortunately for Henry Blogg and a lot of people he saved in later years, there was not much!

The second H. F. Bailey (1924–35) and her crew on the slipway. The boathouse had been built in 1923 to house a motor lifeboat and overcome the difficulties of launching from the beach.

But if he was not a handyman in the house he knew what he liked in the way of interior decoration and furniture. Some of the pieces of furniture he bought from auctions and dealers were very good and he collected valuable French clocks, good oil paintings, mostly sea- or land-scapes, and wall plates.

It was during the First World War that he acquired several pieces of furniture when moving into Swallow Cottage, his new home in a cul-de-sac called Corner Street, just one minute from his favourite lookout on the cliffs and a stone's throw from the church tower. It was a good house but hardly the accepted idea of a fisherman's cottage. The hall parted the living and front rooms. A kitchen with hot water geyser and good fittings was added by Henry Blogg; it gave access through a sliding door to a large store and coal-shed where he kept many of his crab-pots on racks.

The living room had a large blue-tiled fireplace and a fender full of shining brass ornaments. The walls were cleverly painted halfway up to resemble wood panelling and for the rest the pattern on the paper was hidden by certificates, pictures and a beautiful set of wall plates. From the paper-covered ceiling hung an unusual ruby-coloured chandelier. There was a writing desk under the street window and a large birdcage in the back window. The two 'budgies' looked out on flint walls, sheds and the backs of boarding houses.

In the parlour was a secretaire, table and sideboard inlaid and embossed with brass. These valuable pieces of French furniture were not seen to their best advantage, for a cloth, draped to the floor, hid the table, and the sideboard was crowded with clocks, ornaments and souvenirs. Dusting, with Ann Blogg, was a long job but a thorough one.

Perhaps Henry Blogg was most proud of a framed embroidered picture of a sailing lifeboat that hung just inside the door. It was beautifully worked; but his pride lay in the fact that Queenie had made it.

There were two large bedrooms and a narrow one in the front, with a landing at the back. His bedroom had a fine bow window, but it looked inland to the woods and hills. The telephone was close by his bed.

Swallow Cottage

Outside, Swallow Cottage was true to its name. Under the wide eaves was a row of swallows' nests as identical as council houses. The upper walls were of cream-coloured roughcast and the woodwork was painted sea green. The two upper bow windows were typical of Cromer architecture. There was a small concreted backyard hemmed in on all sides and no garden. For over thirty years he walked from Swallow Cottage to his lookout on the cliffs and even the hard pavements must have been worn by his countless footsteps.

On November 26, 1917, Henry Blogg went three times to his vantage point through snow and sleet. He saw nothing to disturb him but he was uneasy and, had he but known it, a vessel was already in dire need of him far out on the dark waters. It was the Norwegian steamer *Kronprincess Victoria*. This ship ran on to the Haisborough Sands at 8 p.m. on Monday November 26 in a raging snowstorm, which had reduced visibility to a few yards. The impact of striking the sand and the blows of the seas quickly paralysed the ship. Helpless and battered, the panic stricken crew took to the rigging. There, with the snow covering them and the wind trying to tear them from their precarious hold, they suffered agonies of exposure. A body quickly succumbed and fell off into the sea; the steward, an Icelander, and the boatswain followed some hours later. The captain was next; he became unconscious and just dropped like a stone from the rigging to the deck, which was awash. The chief engineer, who had held out all those agonised hours, fell into the sea just ten minutes before the lifeboat arrived. Had he but seen the welcome boat he might have found the strength to cling on for those last few minutes.

It was 3.30 a.m. on Tuesday when the *Louisa Heartwell* was launched; and the doomed ship had already been over seven hours on the sands. The wind had dropped considerably but it was still difficult to get the boat away in what was termed a 'moderate' sea. The first launcher to arrive was 'Gillie' Rook, an old lifeboat-man of over ninety. Despite the cold, the darkness and the early hour he was there to help get the boat away. His tracks through the snow would have made the subject for a painting on man's humanity to man.

The snow had stopped, but Henry Blogg had scant information about the location of the vessel and they searched through two bleak, dark hours before deciding to anchor until daylight. But the anchor would not hold, so they kept beating about for the wreck. When day broke cold and cheerless over a dreary sea, they hunted over the sands, sighting many old rusting, gull-fouled wrecks on the Middle Haisbro', but not the one for which they were searching.

After so many hours Henry Blogg felt this must be written off as just another of the scores of fruitless searches he had notched up in his experience and they turned for home. It was a long, hard pull back to Cromer, but luckily the SS *Jarrex* of Hull saw them and, passing a line, towed them nearly home. The many welcome tows given to the row-and-sail lifeboats tell of the sailors' regard for the stalwarts of the RNLI.

Meanwhile at Cromer more information had come in at 7 a.m. from the light-vessel and had wireless then been in use, many an aching arm and back would have been eased. The message said that men had been seen in the rigging of a wrecked steamer five miles south-east of the light-vessel. When, through telescopes, the lifeboat was seen pulling away from the *Jarrex* it was 12.40 p.m. and it was guessed they had not found the wreck, so some fishermen launched a crab-boat and met them with the message.

After hours of hunting about the sands they were now needed almost in the area they had painfully searched! Such were the vexations of the service. The remarks of the crew need drastic expurgation. They were nearly all elderly owing to War claims; they had been soaked to the skin for hours, they were chilled to the marrow and very hungry, but when Henry Blogg asked them individually if they wanted to be relieved they answered, 'No, let's finish the job.'

Although F. H. Barclay had provided food for them at the boathouse, they would not stop but put about and headed back to the sands. That spirit of selflessness is beyond all praise.

The *Louisa Heartwell* showed her fine sailing qualities to the crowd who had gathered, for she covered the thirteen miles back to the sands in sixty-five minutes, which is not bad time for motor-lifeboats.

At 2 p.m. the light-vessel telephoned the shore to say men could still be seen in the steamer's rigging, but the wind was freshening and it was getting really rough on the sands.

There was nothing further they could do at Cromer for their tired men were then well on the way. Within half an hour of that message the lifeboat dropped anchor to windward and veered

Back from the rescue. Henry Blogg, in later years known throughout the country, poses for a photo at the door of the pier boathouse.

down to the wreck, making the boat fast by a grapnel thrown into the mainmast rigging. Once alongside the submerged ship, the crew were able to take   offthesixexhaustedsurvivors.Thesea was then halfway up the masts and three-quarters of the way up the funnel. The four Norwegians and two Danes rescued had been clinging to the rigging in that bitter weather for nineteen hours.

It was a backbreaking pull back to Cromer; no sixty-five-minute sail this time and no tow. When they got off the town every man was utterly exhausted. But there was a welcome home. At 7 p.m. the rumour ran across the town like wildfire that the boat was off the pier and crowds hurried to the beach to see the heroes of the *Fernebo* come in. They saw the brilliant green light of the lifeboat coming inshore and the moonlight was sufficient to show that the lifeboat had more than its crew on board. Ringing cheers went up all along the front and from over the waters came back the faint answering cheer of tired men who knew despite their fatigue and numbness they had done their duty. The 'old men' of Cromer had written another fine chapter in the history of their station and while the rescued men were given treatment for their severe exposure the crew rid themselves of their wet clothes, enjoyed hot food, their own firesides and the satisfaction of a job well done. Human life was cheap just then on the Somme, but on Haisborough Sands it kept its true value and was worth the risk and the labour.

6

The *Georgia*

CROMER WENT as wild with joy as any place in the kingdom when the Armistice of 1918 was signed. Her sons
returned from the shell-scarred fields where the Flanders pop-
pies blew to the peaceful loveliness of their own Poppyland. In
time the lifeboat crew regained some of its younger members
who had been on war service and the aged heroes of the *Fernebo*
rescue gave up their lifebelts for a pipe, a yarn and a fishing-line
on the pier.

To Henry Blogg the post-war years were uneventful compared with the many dramatic calls during hostilities, but in 1920
the Cromer boat rendered one of the longest lifeboat services on
record to the 2500-ton SS *Inverawe* of Sunderland loaded with
phosphate. After she had stranded on the Haisborough Sands on
October 10, six tugs tried to haul the steamer clear. The Cromer
and Palling lifeboats assisted by passing over tows and standing
by. The Cromer boat was launched at 8 p.m. on Sunday and
did not return until Thursday morning, but the grounded ship
was refloated after jettisoning part of her cargo. At one time the
tide was so low that the lifeboatmen got out and walked on the
sands.

In 1923, a new £30,000 boathouse and slipway was built at the
end of the pier. This was a tremendous advance for it permitted
launches in all seas, but there was a big snag – although the boat

could get away in the roughest seas, it could not get back in a heavy sea and had to seek shelter in the nearest harbour, usually Gorleston. The first motor lifeboat, the £10,500 Norfolk-and-Suffolk type *H. F. Bailey*, was housed in the new boathouse and Cromer became a two-boat station, the *Louisa Heartwell* becoming No. 2 boat.

The following year Henry Blogg received from King George V at Buckingham Palace the medal of the Order of the British Empire in recognition of his lifeboat work. With tender pride Ann Blogg placed the new decoration in its velvet-lined case beside Henry's Gold Medal and tried in vain to get him to tell her the hundred and one details she wanted to know about the investiture. 'What did the King say to you? What was he wearing?' Henry Blogg never answered. All he would say was that he was glad to be home!

The early twenties were quiet years for the lifeboat and in 1926 there were only two launches, with no life saved. This, however, was a subdued prelude for the event-filled year of 1927 and

The second H. F. Bailey lifeboat (1924–35). Henry Blogg is at the wheel at the stern as the lifeboat goes under Cromer pier.

Henry Blogg, who liked reading horoscopes and almanacs fore-
telling events, ought to have read, 'The coming year will bring
you world-wide fame and make you the leading lifeboat coxswain.'

The last three months of 1927 will long be remembered for
the violence of the storms that broke over the British Isles and
the mountainous seas that battered the coast, bringing havoc and
shipwreck in their train. On the East Coast three lifeboats wrote
such a brilliant page of combined heroism and self-sacrifice as
has only been matched in the service to the *Rohilla* in 1914. They
all converged on one ship, the SS *Georgia*. This was Henry Blogg's
second spectacular and truly great rescue. It sent his name ringing like a trumpet call round the world.

The *Georgia*, a 389-foot-long Dutch oil tanker of Rotterdam,
was carrying a cargo of crude oil from Abadan to Grangemouth.
She went aground off the South Haisborough Sands, seven miles
north-north-west of the Newarp light-ship, during a heavy gale
about midnight on Sunday November 20, 1927. The trouble
started when her steering gear jammed; heavy seas caught the
unmanageable ship and flung her on to those treacherous sands
with such fury that the tanker immediately broke her back. The
tumult of wind and wave was drowned in the rending of iron
and wood as the vessel split in two. It happened so quickly that
the wireless operator had no time to radio an SOS before the
wireless masts were down and the after part of the *Georgia* was
drifting away from the rest of the ship, which was held fast by
the sandbank. Unlike the *Fernebo*, when all the crew had gathered
on one part of the broken vessel, the crew of the *Georgia* had sixteen men on the half drifting towards the coast and fifteen on the
stranded half.

The after-part of the *Georgia* was caught by the wind, which
was increasing until a full gale, with gusts of fifty miles an hour,
was blowing from east by south, and by the heavy seas, so that
the rolling, pitching wreck was carried to the north-west. The
men on board clung grimly to their helpless half-ship as the seas
struck her again and again and, through the wild darkness of the

night, swept over her decks. It was a terrifying experience – the frenzied elements, the banging and rattling of loose metal and timber where the ship had been torn and the violent, drunken rolling in those great billows. Hour after hour the crew endured until the slow dawn showed the damage that had been wrought by wind and sea.

With red swollen eyes bleared by salt spray they looked over the tormented waters for a sign of land. They saw nothing but dirty clouds lowering to monstrous seas whose smoking crests were flung forward by the gale. For what seemed eternity the hulk lurched through the raging seas. Midday came and the afternoon dragged by. Then, when the sixteen men began to feel their plight was helpless, a cry went up from a man near the funnel, 'Ship in sight.'

Through the flurry of spray the others peered eastward until they could see the smoke and dark blur of a ship. It was the SS *Trent*, and her master brought the vessel as near as he could to the rolling after-part of the *Georgia* and got a line across her. One by one the seamen left the wreck and were hauled on board the *Trent*. The hulk drifted shoreward and finally foundered off Cromer. The rescued seamen at once told the master of the *Trent* about their comrades stranded on the sands and he put back against the heavy sea to the east, where the crew thought the other half of the *Georgia* had been left. At the same time he sent a wireless message to the shore stating that help was urgently needed to get men off the wrecked *Georgia*.

Meanwhile Captain Kissing of the *Georgia* kept sounding a distress signal. He had also burnt flares through the previous night until none was left. Forty-eight flares lit up the sinister water breaking on the sands, revealing the plight of the mutilated ship, but so inky was the night that not one was seen either by the light-vessel or coastguards on the shore.

The wireless message from the *Trent* was picked up and passed to the Great Yarmouth and Gorleston lifeboat station and the motor-lifeboat *John and Mary Meiklam* was launched at 8.30 p.m. on Monday.

It was a vile night, a full gale, a heavy sea and bitterly cold, but in less than two hours the lifeboat reached the scene of the wreck and found the *Trent* standing by, half a mile from the *Georgia*. She could get no nearer the stranded vessel without grave risk. Her master told coxswain William Fleming that he had rescued the sixteen men from the other half of the *Georgia*. He felt that conditions were too bad to do anything here in the dark and counselled the lifeboat to stand by throughout the night and attempt a rescue in the morning.

The *Trent* fired several signals but there was no answer from the wreck. No sign of life at all. It looked as if in the darkness the men left behind had been claimed by the hungry waters. Coxswain Fleming agreed to stand by and the *Trent* passed a hawser to hold the lifeboat in the violent seas that were running on the sands. This permitted prompt action if the state of the wrecked vessel became desperate and there were signs of survivors. The crew of the lifeboat kept ceaseless watch for signals from the wreck while keeping their boat head on to the waves.

Slowly, through hours of strain and anxiety, the terrible night dragged by. The crew had been wet through almost from the time they set out. It was painfully cold and they were hungry.

When the grey November dawn strengthened, the men who had maintained their watch saw the pitiable condition of the *Georgia*, with great seas rushing at her and crashing in clouds of spray right over her upper decks.

When the light was strong enough the master of the *Trent* prepared to heave anchor and go in as close as he dare, hoping that this would give a lee to the lifeboat. But fate was still against them. A mist came down so quickly that it hid the wreck almost as completely as the curtain of darkness. So the *Trent* waited until the mist had lifted. The lifeboat then worked round into position and anchored in the lee of the steamer. But though they were as close as they dared to go, it was not enough. Enormous seas were rearing and sweeping over the upper bridge of the wreck where the crew could now be seen huddled for shelter.

Coxswain Fleming realised that nothing he could do would

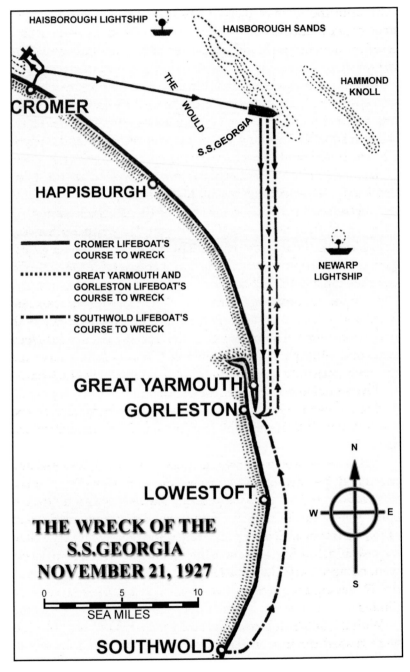

HAISBOROUGH LIGHTSHIP

HAISBOROUGH SANDS

HAMMOND KNOLL

CROMER

THE WOULD

S.S.GEORGIA

HAPPISBURGH

CROMER LIFEBOAT'S COURSE TO WRECK

GREAT YARMOUTH AND GORLESTON LIFEBOAT'S COURSE TO WRECK

SOUTHWOLD LIFEBOAT'S COURSE TO WRECK

NEWARP LIGHTSHIP

GREAT YARMOUTH
GORLESTON

LOWESTOFT

THE WRECK OF THE
S.S.GEORGIA
NOVEMBER 21, 1927

0   5   10
SEA MILES

N
W   E
S

SOUTHWOLD

avail until the force of the tide abated; probably the change of tide would moderate those murderous breakers. So the lifeboat weighed anchor and stood out farther from the sandbank, waiting for the change of tide.

At noon she again approached the *Georgia,* anchored in the lee of the *Trent,* and tried with her line-throwing gun to make communication with the wreck. Two, three, four lines were fired without success. Then, when it began to appear that this method was useless, one line went right across the wreck from sixty yards distance. The expectant crew on the *Georgia* caught the line and hastily secured it. But cruel ill luck was dogging both lifeboat and distressed men, for a titanic wave like a mad roaring monster came down over the wreck. It lifted and then dropped the lifeboat and swept the line to leeward, putting such a strain upon it that the stout rope, two inches in circumference, was broken; the last rope the lifeboat had!

Despair, with fingers colder than that icy wind, gripped rescuers and wrecked seamen. It seemed that fate, in league with that brutal sea, was working for their deaths. The lifeboat-men were now utterly exhausted. They had had no food apart from the emergency rations of biscuits and tinned meat which the coxswain had doled out with some Navy rum.

The coxswain, realising his men were all in, hove anchor and made to the HMS *Thanet,* a destroyer from Chatham, which had arrived.

Hot tea was procured from the destroyer, which warmed and heartened the men of the *John and Mary Meiklam.* The lifeboat motor had given trouble and fresh water was supplied for the circulating system. For twenty minutes the lifeboat remained astern of the destroyer and, after promising its commanding officer that they would return at daybreak for another attempt, the crew went home to Gorleston, reaching their base at 6 p.m. on November 22, having been twenty-two hours at sea in most severe conditions.

With the failure to rescue the seamen, Board of Trade officials were rushed down from London by car with a special rocket-firing pistol which had a range of 300 yards. It was put on the *Elizabeth Simpson*, a volunteer lifeboat of Gorleston, at 7.30 p.m. on Tuesday and the Dutch owner of the *Georgia*, M. Hoinke, who was in London, went with the boat to give the position of the oil-containers to avoid undue risk of fire when releasing the rocket. But the attempt was unsuccessful.

At 2.15 p.m. on November 21, five hours before the *John and Mary Meiklam* had gone out, Henry Blogg had seen from his vantage-point on the cliff-top what he took to be a large steamship in bad condition four miles north-east of Cromer. Its bows seemed completely under water, but the funnel and mainmast clearly showed. Below him the breakers, riding in from hundreds of miles of sea, were bursting against the groynes and sea walls like thunder, crashing over the promenade and pier and for a hundred yards out to sea there was a white mass of foam and surf.

The alarm was given and lifeboat-men came running from all parts of the town to the boat-house on the pier. The wooden doors were folded back and the crew struggled into their gear. Then the release-pins were knocked from the bow- and stern-chains and, with Henry Blogg gripping his spoked wheel and shouting orders to the crew, the *H. F. Bailey* slithered with increasing speed down its greased slipway into the sea.

They made for the vessel but found on reaching it that it was only half a ship and there appeared to be no one on board. After making as sure as possible that the wreck was deserted Henry Blogg returned to Cromer to see if there was any news from Haisbro' light-vessel. It was then 3.15 a.m. and the seas were so heavy that it was impossible to get back up the slipway. The coxswain at first decided to run down the coast to Yarmouth and wait there for the storm to abate, but on reflection he considered the wreck to be such a danger to shipping that it was his duty to remain by her throughout the night in spite of the fearful weather.

It was no easy decision to make in view of the intense cold and appalling conditions, but nevertheless he took the lifeboat back to the deserted portion of the *Georgia* and stayed by her throughout the long, wild night. Away to the south-east the Gorleston boat was standing by the other half of the broken ship.

When daylight came Henry Blogg had done his duty as far as the wreck was concerned, and after sixteen hours he returned to his station and waited the opportunity to get housed while the reserve lifeboat *Louisa Heartwell* took over his watch at the wreck.

While the *H. F. Bailey* was riding on the housing-buoy at the end of the slipway, the coastguard brought news from Bacton that a small boat with one man in her had been seen drifting towards the shore.

The crew and coxswain were looking forward to a hot meal and dry clothes after that rigorous night's watch, but a life was in peril and straightway Henry Blogg cast off and turned south.

When off Bacton Henry Blogg caught sight of a small boat on a wave's crest in the boiling surf. Anxiously he peered at it for several minutes and satisfied himself that it was empty. A deserted half-ship and an empty boat were not much reward for what they had endured!

Once more the coxswain put the boat and hungry, worn-out crew towards Cromer. It was past midday when they again arrived off the slipway and arranged to get the boat up. This was no easy manoeuvre. The lifeboat has to be secured by two ropes to a buoy west of the slipway and with the tide running east the ropes are allowed to run out to bring the boat opposite and in line with the slipway. A hawser from the power-driven winch is then secured to stern-ropes and, after two balancing ropes have been secured on either side of the slipway, the lifeboat is hauled up. While this rather delicate manoeuvre was in progress the propeller got fouled and the crew were busy clearing it when F. H. Barclay, the secretary, arrived panting at the top of the slipway. He told Henry Blogg that a telegram had come from the head office in London, ordering his boat to the Haisborough Sands to reinforce the Great Yarmouth and Gorleston boat.

There was no room to argue. The looked-for hot meal, the dry clothes, the rest and the hot drinks must be denied. It was tough but there was a duty to be done. Neither Henry Blogg nor his crew had so much as a thought that in turning back to that angry sea again, after nearly a day and a night without rest, they were going to achieve one of the finest rescues in the annals of their service. As the wife of the secretary said later, 'It made us all feel inches taller because we belonged to the same town as they did.'

So while the reserve boat *Louisa Heartwell* stood by the after part of the *Georgia*, the *H. F. Bailey* began her third mission heading for the Haisborough Sands.

The position of the wreck had been clearly given and although the crew groused and swore with many a fisherman's oath about the interfering folk at head office and bemoaned the hot meal and sleep they had lost, not one of them would have turned back or said they would not go to reinforce coxswain Fleming's men.

A good grouse does a world of good in such conditions and Henry Blogg grinned to himself as he heard his men letting off steam while he fought to keep the stout boat head-on to those dangerous seas. Through the mist of icy spray that stung his face like a whip he peered ahead for signs of a broken ship.

His keen eyes roved from sea to compass and from compass round the boat to the crew with some anxiety. It was tough on these men – twenty-six hours of heavy toil and ceaseless vigil in this roaring gale, under terrible conditions of cold. But they would not let him down and he must not let them down. So much depended on his judgement and seamanship: their lives, his own and, it may be, the men on the wreck. He too was feeling the strain of those long hours of struggle and the grave responsibility. He would be glad when this exacting service was over, but that would not be yet awhile.

Suddenly he stiffened as his sharp, experienced eyes saw a blur in the distance that he knew to be a ship. He yelled against the clamour of the storm to Jack Davies, his bowman, and most of the crew peered too in that direction, one by one confirming what the coxswain had seen.

It was 4.15 p.m. The November day was merging into a brief twilight and darkness.

Now Henry Blogg began to take stock of the situation as he

neared the sands. He gazed all round for a boat or a light but there was no sign of the Great Yarmouth and Gorleston crew. As he ran closer to the *Georgia* he saw that matters were desperate aboard the storm-battered hulk. The seas were much worse on the sand than in deeper water; big waves were breaking right over the upper bridge where the men were crouched, half dead with cold and cruel exposure and even if the ship did not soon go to pieces those men could not endure much more. The gathering gloom made matters even more pressing. The longer he waited the less chance of getting them off. He could anchor and use his line-throwing gun to get a line aboard, but that would take time – and time was not on their side.

One great advantage was theirs. One of the huge oil tanks had burst and hundreds of tons of oil had poured out on to the sea on the lee side of the wreck. Here was a non-recurring chance, but one which needed great courage to grasp. Henry Blogg surveyed and summed up the situation and in a few minutes decided that – in spite of the grave danger to himself, his crew and his boat – here was a chance that held the promise of succouring those fifteen unknown men of that doomed ship. Without hesitation or vacillation he seized it.

Was it possible that the placid-looking fisherman with a nose like a Roman emperor, who stood with a basket of towels outside a tent-hiring hut on the promenade with his hands in his front pockets and his cap pulled down over his eyes, was the man who now stood at the helm and drove the *H. F. Bailey* straight to the wreck, over the sandbank, over hidden pieces of wreckage that could rip the bottom out of his boat and through that terrible sea that was beating to death in a white fury its latest victim?

With a skill that would otherwise have made this manoeuvre suicidal, Henry Blogg took his boat through the oil-patch right alongside the battered *Georgia*.

'I'm going alongside,' he yelled.

His crew, without further instructions, knew what they had to do and knew almost as well as he did the risk he was taking, yet they concurred.

Every man was at his post, the bowman ready with weighted hand-line grimly holding to the rails and ready to fling that line at the precise moment.

Now Henry Blogg had got the boat right alongside. The line, flung with desperate urgency and splendid aim, snaked out towards the group of men on the bridge. The half-frozen men, buoyed with new hope as they saw the lifeboat coming in towards them, braced themselves to catch it. But even as Jack Davies flung the line a towering sea crashed against the side of the wreck, reared, broke and caught the lifeboat on the rebound, turning it completely round, almost washing the bowman over-board and hurling the boat stern-first against the iron sides of the wreck.

This was the risk that Henry Blogg had taken with his eyes open. This was the sea's answer to such daring.

With a crash that flung Henry Blogg against his wheel and nearly every member of the crew to the deck, the lifeboat hit the wall of iron. Her stern-post was badly smashed, the rudder severely strained and the rear of the boat bashed in. But, fortunately, the rudder still responded to the wheel. Blogg spun the helm frantically and shouted with relief as he felt it respond. He yelled an order above the tumult of the sea and two of the crew grasped his words in a flash and flung other lines up to the men on the wreck.

The shipwrecked men had gasped in horror as they saw the lifeboat flung round and dashed against their ship, but as the lines spun upward from that boat they had the presence of mind to grasp them. Desperately, they fastened them, while on the life-boat they had been whipped round a bollard. The lifeboat was now moored to the wreck. The calamity had been a blessing in disguise. By seizing an opportunity flung at them in the midst of what seemed disaster they had achieved their purpose.

Henry Blogg shouted, 'Take your time: Be steady and jump one at a time.'

The crew formed into line, the youngest first and Captain Kissing last. Two Dutch sailors suddenly dashed out of the queue to try and save the ship's mascot – a black cat – but they could not. They had previously tried to save two hens in a coop, but these were washed away.

Without delay, in ones and twos, the half-frozen seamen jumped the ten feet into the lifeboat as it rose on the crest of each wave. The cook of the *Georgia* had bought three Persian rugs while in the Persian Gulf, as a Christmas present for his mother. He salvaged them from his berth and kept them with him while huddled in the fo'c'sle and the bridge and before he jumped into the lifeboat he wrapped them round him – they acted as padding as well as keeping him warm later!

In three drama-filled minutes the fifteen exhausted men had all got into the lifeboat; and at a triumphant shout from Henry Blogg, 'Cut the lines, Jack!' the two mooring ropes were severed. The eighty-horse-power engine roared and the bow was turned to get away from the wreck. But, as if in fury at such successful temerity, the North Sea flung a vast wave at the boat. It was as though a moving cliff of water bore down upon them. It snatched up the eighteen-ton boat as though but a straw and lifted her right on to the bulwarks of the wreck. For half a minute it seemed this was the end; the boat must be smashed like an eggshell. But even in that dread moment of disaster Robert Davies, with the reputation of one of the best fishermen-engineers in the lifeboat service, kept his head. Without waiting for an order he promptly reversed his engine and fortunately there was enough water for the propeller to drag the lifeboat off.

It is a feature of a lifeboat engine that it can go straight from full ahead to full astern. That instantaneous action, with engine roaring at full power, saved them. Henry Blogg spun the wheel like a madman and yelled, 'Full speed ahead, Bob.' The bows came round and the damaged boat was clear of the wreck. As it was, the fore-part of the bilge-keel had been torn off, a jagged hole was made in the starboard side of the fore compartment and the lifeboat was waterlogged. Twice in a few minutes the boat and crew had almost met with disaster and twice in that time quick action, brilliant seamanship and their team spirit had saved them. Every one of that stout-hearted crew licked his salty lips with relief when they were through that crisis. Not one of them had been nearer destruction than they were in those last few minutes. Henry Blogg had taken a great risk to achieve a great end and one of the finest crews a coxswain could wish for had shared the risk and helped him to achieve success. As Lord Templewood said of him, 'He inspired the fullest confidence in his crew. They would follow him anywhere for they knew he had the courage to face disaster and the skill to surmount it.'

The rescued seamen were in a pathetic state. They had had no food for forty hours as their mess-room had been on the other half of the ship, and the fumes from the oil had been almost unbearable. They lay in the cabin of the lifeboat red-eyed and blue with cold, their hands and faces raw and swollen. Already one of the lifeboat-men was passing round the flask of rum as Henry Blogg turned the boat due south for the Cockle Gat and Yarmouth Road.

Captain Kissing had been very anxious about the rest of his crew on the other half of the ship and was greatly relieved when he was told they were safe.

The coxswain did not want to strain his damaged boat further and tried to maintain a moderate speed, but the tide-stream and a following wind hurried them to Yarmouth, plunging into heavy seas all the way.

Henry Blogg felt severely the fatigue and strain of the last two hours and George Balls, second coxswain, helped him at the wheel. The relief he experienced as he turned away from that dead ship that had twice nearly broken his boat was immense. His boldness had almost meant disaster and yet by a hair's breadth he had snatched a great victory.

The Cromer boat put into Gorleston about 6.30 p.m. The rescued seamen and the exhausted lifeboat-men, who had been out for twenty-eight hours, were given every attention. The crew rested there that night and took their boat home next day – arriving at 1 p.m. A great crowd had gathered on the pier to welcome them, or, as the local paper said, 'Cromer is the proudest town in the kingdom this week.' The cliffs and beach resounded with cheers as the *H. F. Bailey* came to the slipway, curtseying as if in acknowledgement of the welcome. The pier had been thrown open and 2000 people crowded on to it. Behind them from the stately tower of the church came the joyous pealing of bells. Then two maroons boomed overhead – the coastguard was paying his tribute too.

Alderman D. Davison, Chairman of the Cromer UDC, was on the concrete slipway to welcome the crew. As Henry Blogg saw the army of admirers to be faced he said, 'I'd rather be home out of this.' But first there was a speech of welcome and loud cheers, including 'One for the boys' – the five youngsters in the crew. Then ladies gave the younger men boxes of chocolates and as the crew made their way through the throng they were patted on the back and even kissed.

It is not on record that Henry Blogg received any of the latter attentions, but when he was climbing the cliff gangway his wife met him and said, 'Henry, you're blushing like a kid!'

'Ah, I know,' said her husband, 'and I feel like one.'

So perhaps he had been among the favoured ones! Later that day when the Press asked for a report Henry Blogg said, 'What's all the fuss about? We have to do it.'

But the story does not end there.

This service was unique in the annals of our lifeboats, for another gallant coxswain and crew added to that magnificent display of courage and seamanship. This time it is the Southwold boat that sets the blood tingling; the Southwold crew, fifteen miles below Yarmouth, had been instructed from head office at 1.15 p.m. that day that the Lowestoft boat, which should have gone out, had been damaged in a heroic service to the *Lily of Devon*, a sailing smack, so they must make their way to the Haisborough Sands to relieve the Yarmouth boat after first embarking oil at Gorleston.

From Southwold coxswain Frank Upcraft hurried northward past Pakefield and Lowestoft to Gorleston. After taking on the oil and W. C. Johnson, a drifter-skipper who knew the dreaded sands (for the Southwold boat was far out of its area) and Captain Carver, the district inspector of lifeboats, coxswain Upcraft headed out through the Roads, past Scroby Sands to the scene of the wreck. In doing so he actually passed Henry Blogg in the darkness, coming south with the entire crew from the forepart of the wreck. But coxswain Upcraft pressed on to the wreck and, arriving there, found HMS *Thanet* still standing by, also unaware that in the gloom the Cromer boat had taken off the crew. The lifeboat asked her for information of any survivors and the destroyer turned her searchlights on the wreck in a careful examination. There was no sign of life. Captain Carver and coxswain Upcraft decided, however, that they must make absolutely sure. To do this meant running right up to the wreck. So at 9.15 p.m., in the darkness of that November night, with her own searchlight and the destroyer's focused on the *Georgia*, the Southwold crew got as close as they dare, anxiously scanning every part of the flooded deck. Then, in a moment of comparative calm, they ran the lifeboat almost alongside to make absolutely sure they could turn back knowing there was no more to be done. In doing so they too almost met disaster for a huge sea suddenly lunged at the boat, completely engulfing her. Captain Carver was standing with his arms gripped round the mizzen-mast when the sea hit them. The lifeboat heeled right over to an angle of forty-five degrees and when she righted herself he seemed to be clinging to a mast sticking out of a seething mass of water. He could not see another member of the crew or anything else of the lifeboat!

When the Southwold lifeboat reached Yarmouth she had been out thirteen hours.

Commenting on coxswain Upcraft's determination, Henry Blogg said, 'That was one of the most heroic deeds I have heard of. I know only too well what those Southwold men must have had to endure.'

Through that fierce gale three boats had gone to aid the fifteen men on the fore-part of the *Georgia*; the Great Yarmouth and Gorleston boat had been out twenty-two hours, Southwold thirteen hours and the Cromer boat twenty-eight hours. The Gorleston men had been thwarted by the bitter cold and storm. As coxswain Fleming said, 'What could I do? We were all finished and half dead.' The Southwold crew, rather than chance leaving one poor wretch on that sea-swept wreck, had risked destruction. And Henry Blogg, in twenty-eight hours battling with the sea, had stood by the deserted after-part of the *Georgia* and the little storm-tossed boat and had gone in to make one of the most daring rescues on record.

The RNLI awarded Henry Blogg his second Gold Medal, and first to congratulate him were the coxswain and the crew of the Great Yarmouth boat. The last time a man had won the Gold Medal of the Institution twice for actual services was in 1848.

William Fleming added a Silver Medal to his Gold and Bronze Medals and coxswain Upcraft got a Bronze Medal. Each member of the Cromer crew got the Bronze Medal and the Great Yarmouth crew the thanks of the Institution on vellum and the Southwold crew an additional monetary award.

The crew of the *H. F. Bailey* were: George Balls, second cox; John J. Davies, bowman; R. Davies, mechanic; L. Harrison; E. W. Allen; W. T. Davies; J. W. Davies; H. W. Davies; S. Harrison; R. Barker; G. Cox; J. J. Davies, jun.

After the storm came the calm and the bouquets. A dinner and concert were given in the Newhaven Court Hotel on November 29 and a high tea on December 7. It was in Cromer Town Hall on January 30, 1928, that a packed enthusiastic audience saw Henry Blogg and his team presented with their honours. The vellum recording the award of the clasp to his Gold Medal was presented by George F. Shee, secretary of the RNLI.

A fund had been started for the crew, and the owners of the *Georgia* gave £50 with the suggestion that it should be shared by the crew according to rank, but Henry Blogg said, 'No, share and share alike is the motto of Cromer lifeboat.' Henry Blogg thought if that went for danger it should also go for gifts.

Then Alderman D. Davison read letters of congratulation from other lifeboat stations and presented Henry Blogg with a gold watch and each of the crew with a silver watch.

At the annual general meeting of the RNLI on March 28, in Westminster Central Hall, London, HRH the Prince of Wales, President of the Institution, made the actual award. He also remarked before presenting the award:

> Coxswain Blogg's achievement is one which confers honour not only on himself, not only on the splendid crew which he leads, not even only on the Norfolk stations, which have a magnificent record in the annals of the lifeboat service, but on the lifeboat service, whose spirit he so splendidly embodies and I am sure we shall all join in congratulating him on the unique distinction.

> But there is one little habit which I feel that coxswain Blogg should break himself of; and I am sure if there are any ship-owners or marine underwriters here they would like me to bring this to his notice. Apparently he seems to regard it as an indispensable condition of the highest exercise of his seamanship, at any rate in gold medal cases, that the vessel must break in two. In the case of the *Fernebo* in January 1917, that vessel broke in two, each part floating away and coming to rest a mile or so apart on the rocks off Cromer, where Blogg rescued the crew of eleven after three heroic attempts in the pulling boat. In the case of the *Georgia*, I notice that the vessel took care to follow the same procedure and therefore received Blogg's immediate attention. I know that he will always be ready to launch his boat to the assistance of any vessel in distress and I can only suggest to him that he should not be too particular as to the precise number of pieces into which the wreck divides itself.

7

The Roughest Trip

THE GREAT service to the *Georgia* was followed a month later by the worst trip that Henry Blogg ever made – sixty-five miles in the wildest sea they had known, on a wild goose chase to the *Crawford Castle*. It was the only time the Cromer lifeboat was reported missing and a voyage no man could forget. Yet for all they risked and endured, for all the tears of the women-folk, it was for nothing – for they rendered no service to the *Crawford Castle*. But perhaps it was not in vain, for the dangers and rigours of that wild journey welded the crew even more tightly together and demonstrated again the amazing seamanship of Henry Blogg, strengthening the growing tradition of the Cromer station.

Christmas week 1927 was a busy one for the lifeboat service. There were twenty launches in that week of gales and most of them were on the east and south coasts. The Great Yarmouth and Gorleston boat went out four times on December 21. The storms did subside for a day or two, then on Christmas night they sprang up with added violence.

Not only was the gale at full strength but with the wind came snow, piling into deep drifts that isolated many villages inland and caused anxiety about supplies. Telegraph poles were blown down around the coast and communication was cut in many places. Gale damage and havoc made up most of the news.

While most of Cromer was enjoying the festivities behind stout walls, the men whose duty kept them from their own firesides, even on Christmas Day, were keeping anxious watch out to sea, for this gale had no goodwill for seamen. At 9 p.m. when the party fun was at its height, Haisbro' light-vessel reported disturbing news to the Cromer coastguard and he in turn hastily consulted Henry Blogg. The SS *Crawford Castle* of the Union Castle Line, 2820 tons, in ballast, had been in collision with the light vessel and in view of the fierce east-north-east gale and exceptionally heavy seas the lifeboat might be needed at any moment.

When Henry Blogg heard the message he rang Daniel Davison who was acting for the secretary and they agreed the crew should be warned at once and assembled in case of an urgent call. So the games were interrupted in half a dozen homes and the laughter stopped when a heavy urgent knock was heard at the door and the news given. Pandemonium reigned for a few minutes; then, when husband or father had gone in a whirl of overcoats and sea-boots, some tried to restart the fun. But the shadow was there – the shadow that falls on the homes of the lifeboat crew when the call of duty comes on nights like this.

Puffing and panting, the twelve men gathered in the boathouse at the end of the pier that rocked with the wind's violence. So thunderous was the sea beneath the concrete floor that ordinary talk was impossible. But as they waited with their boat gleaming and ready for the launch, they shouted questions about the parties they had left, the Christmas dinner, the beer and the state of the tide. Henry Blogg sat silent near the telephone-box, waiting for further news from the light-vessel.

The long wait in the bitter cold with that sea roaring beneath and around might well have made Henry Blogg wish himself out of the lifeboat service. But it did not. As he had said to a lifeboat inspector, 'It's not us, sir, it's those men out there.'

He did not think of what he was missing or enduring or risking, but of what others were suffering. That remained true for his fifty years of lifeboat service and was the hall-mark of his greatness. He showed that nobility of character in his face.

At 10.15 p.m. the coastguard rang: the light-vessel had reported it had sustained slight damage in the collision. The steamer, however, was two miles to the north-west and was showing 'out of control' lights. It appeared to be drifting towards shallow water.

That was not too cheerful, so Henry Blogg kept the crew at stand-by until 11.30 p.m., waiting above the sea and beneath the boat for the call that did not come. Just what was happening out there to the unmanageable ship in the storm they could not know, but they were not yet requested. As there was no further message it was decided to dismiss the crew and the coastguard said he would let them know immediately there was any worsening of the situation.

The Davies, Harrisons, 'Boy Primo' Allen, Robert Cox and Henry Blogg went home and, if the party was still going, joined in the rest of the games or went to bed to get what sleep they could in case of an early-morning call.

Long before daylight on that rough Boxing Day Henry Blogg enquired for further news. The weather was in no way sorry for its unchristian behaviour on Christmas Day; if anything, its mood was more truculent. The 8 o'clock news told of high winds lashing the whole country and spoke of further heavy snowfalls. Well, it was a holiday and one did not have to go out of doors!

It was not until 11.10 a.m. on that aptly named Boxing Day that action was required. The *Crawford Castle* was still out of control but was near the East Dudgeon light vessel, thirty miles farther north. She was, however, now asking for lifeboat and tug assistance.

That put an end to the period of waiting. The maroons cracked and in almost record time the crew arrived. The *H. F. Bailey* was quickly launched into a terrific sea. Alec Jackson saw the boat speed at thirty miles an hour down the slipway and the tremendous sea rear up over her as she was launched. He saw Henry Blogg, gripping the wheel, bend forward into the wall of water as a bather might plunge into the sea. His heart missed a beat as he felt sure some of the crew would be washed overboard, but the sea swept on and he saw every man clinging for life but still in the boat. That frightening start was the keynote of the whole voyage. Fortunately the lifeboat was the Watson cabin type, for had it been an open boat like the famous Norfolk-and-Suffolk type, then the crew would have been washed right out of her as she plunged down the slipway into those rearing waves. Every man was soaked almost as soon as the boat was afloat.

George Balls, second coxswain, joined Henry Blogg at the helm to keep the boat steady in the seas that went right over them as they turned and headed north for the long run to the Dudgeon light-vessel. They adopted the unusual practice of standing each side of the wheel, facing one another so that they could see the seas coming both fore and aft.

The *H. F. Bailey* was not a quarter of a mile away from the slipway when a further message came through, passed on by the Haisbro' light-vessel, saying the steamer was under control and proceeding on its way. The coastguard immediately ran up the recall signal, but so bad was the weather and thick the air with spindrift and spray that the crew never saw it, but kept on their way climbing the hills of green water and dipping into the valleys, standing at times almost on end, so steep were the waves.

The crew were already drenched to the skin and for the rest of that long journey they knew intense discomfort. The splendid boat battled every yard of the way with scuppers constantly working and icy spray and spume flying over her continuously. Every twenty minutes or so she took green seas on board, which completely buried her. The waves swept from end to end, filling the cockpit and causing every man to hang on grimly for life itself. The valves worked so efficiently, however, that the seas were rapidly cleared.

So, for mile after mile, the crew fought seas unparalleled in their experience, until they reached the position in which the steamer was expected. It could not be seen, so they began searching for a ship that, unbeknown to them, had gone on its way, if not rejoicing, at least very relieved. Henry Blogg and the bowman peered in vain through a mist of salt spray with the wind as sharp as a knife. Then the coxswain decided to talk to the light vessel. They carried on a little farther and the master of the vessel reported that the steamer had nearly collided with him in the darkness before 6 a.m. and he had burned a couple of flares in warning. The *Crawford Castle* was apparently taking a tilt at light-vessels! He had last seen the ship going north under its own power about 10.30 a.m.

Well, there it was. They had fought their way for thirty miles in the dirtiest weather they had known and in constant danger of being washed overboard and now they were not needed. The ship was not even there.

There was nothing more they could do except get back home out of this bitter wind and berserk sea and that was not as easy as it sounded. In fact, the sea was so rough and they had come so far north, that it was more practicable to carry on to Grimsby than to turn south for Cromer, which really meant going on to Yarmouth. The trouble was that Henry Blogg had never been in to Grimsby, nor had any of his crew. He had no chart of the coast and it would soon be dark. To enter an unknown river-mouth without chart or pilot, in the dark, in those seas was a tremendous responsibility. The fact that Henry Blogg did it is a remarkable testimony to the man. Jimmy Davies, his nephew, said, 'His navigation was self-taught but I would trust my life to him anywhere.' And that went for every member of the lifeboat crew.

So they brought the bows of the *H. F. Bailey* round for the Humber. In his mind, as the boat climbed and dipped with the great seas lifting and leaving her, the coxswain tried to recall charts he had seen in a nautical almanac at home. At least, his crew have since reasoned, that was the only place he could have gained the layout of buoys and channels. The fact that Henry Blogg had a memory like a camera-plate meant the difference between safety and disaster on that occasion.

As darkness came the situation seemed so serious that the youngest members of the crew (there were three in their teens) were put in the most protected part of the boat, so that if the worst came to the worst and they were hit by one of these seas they would stand the best chance of surviving. Such was the spirit of the crew and such the danger to their lives.

Back at Cromer the hours dragged by without news. Everyone grew more and more anxious. The roar of the sea was so loud and the wind so strong that the most easy-going were shaken. Forebodings of disaster brought the wives and sweethearts of the crew together in their cottages, trying to get news and to comfort one another. Ann Blogg, perhaps because she had known so many anxious hours with her husband as coxswain, was a tower of strength. She maintained that no news was good news – and tried to believe it herself. But Daniel Davison was so anxious that he organised a search-party, which set off in a car despite the gale. They drove along the Sheringham coast-road, searching the shore for the wreck of their lifeboat. Telephone wires and poles were down around the coast; trees and hoardings too had been blown over, but they found no trace of the *H. F. Bailey* which, had they known it, was fifty miles away, struggling to make the Humber. As the hours dragged by without news the earlier fears that the worst had happened seemed confirmed. The *H. F. Bailey* was missing.

Some thirty years later, on a sunny afternoon with no wind at all, Mrs Jack Davies – now well into her seventies – recalled those terrible hours of waiting.

'I have never seen the boat go off in worse weather,' she said. 'You could not see it after it entered the water at the end of the pier, there was such a smother of spray.'

'That was the only time I knew my mother to cry,' said one of the crew to me. But she had a son and a husband on that boat!

The women just had to wait, resting on the assurance of the coastguard that as soon as he got any news he would let them know. Nothing more could be done. As one anxious wife hurried through the gale-swept streets to another they put the kettle on and over a cup of tea told each other that everything was all right, while outside the sea boomed in mockery and the wind howled like demons.

The women of Cromer did not assist in launching the boat,

although in earlier years they had done so, but they did what they could to help their men. When Henry Blogg got news of a ship in distress Ann Blogg would fling a coat over her night-dress and run out into the night to knock up other members of the crew. Other women hurried to the boat-house with clothing and saw with tear-blurred eyes their men go out into wild seas. They then turned and went back to the house, perhaps to the children, to do mechanically, hour after hour, the ordinary jobs of the home with their minds all the time out on the waters with their loved one. And as each gust caught the house and the rain lashed the windows they thought of the fury of that sea and that fine, but oh, so little, boat.

No matter what the hour, Ann Blogg never went back to bed after Henry Blogg had gone. She would sit up alone through the night, waiting in case she was needed to answer the telephone and to be ready when her husband got home. The wom-enfolk could not relieve the anxiety of their minds by strenuous action. Theirs was the long, long wait and the gnawing anxiety. Rarely did grateful people mention their part and there were neither medals nor pealing church-bells and no cheers. But no boat would have gone

Ann Blogg admires Henry's George Cross.

had the women failed to play their part – the harder part.

Mrs Henry Davies stood on the cliff one wild day and saw the boat launched with her husband on board. It seemed the boat was standing on end against a mountain of green water and behind that towering wave came another and another, in fearful rapidity. It looked impossible for men to hold on with their boat at such an angle and the waves sweeping on them so fast. She could not believe the boat could live in such seas. People talked to her, but she did not hear them or know who they were. Her hair was blown, her face wet from the driving rain. She could not keep back the tears. She just stood high above the raging sea, watching her husband go out, praying that he should be brought home safely. She stood there, typifying the women of Britain whose men man the lifeboats.

The *H. F. Bailey* reached Grimsby about midnight. Somehow their incomparable coxswain had found the channel and brought them safely into harbour. Not even those who knew him best could really tell how, but he guided them safely into port, utterly exhausted, yet safe, having survived sixty-five miles of the roughest voyage they had ever known.

Jack Davies remembers that, before darkness closed on them and on the wild sea, they saw a great wave strike a large steamer not far from them and sweep right over the bridge.

'Good job we didn't stop that one, George,' commented the coxswain to his helper at the helm.

Worn out, soaked and chilled to the marrow, without the consolation of knowing they had saved even a ship's cat, the crew went ashore. They moored their boat and found the Sailors' Home in the dim-lit streets of the port. Stiff-limbed and sore, with eyes red and inflamed from the lashing of wind and sea and salt glistening on skin and hair, they looked a bedraggled company. But if ever men had earned admiration they had. They had hot baths and were put into whatever dry clothes could be found for them. While they were doing this, Henry Blogg tried again and again to get through to Ann or the coastguard, but the lines were down. So the women had to wait all through that night until the next morning, when the crew, having left their boat with Robert Davies the mechanic, caught an early train at Grimsby. They changed at King's Lynn and at last Henry Blogg managed to get a telephone message through from there. When they bought copies of the local paper they found the headline: Cromer Lifeboat Missing. And they were not surprised.

Through those unending hours of anxiety Ann Blogg had tried to keep up her spirits, but those who knew her realised how worried she had become. She pottered to and fro from kitchen to living-room, trying to be busy but really doing nothing, her mind obviously far away. The relief and joy with which she heard the voice of her husband can be imagined. Then, on flying feet, she went from house to house in that little fishing-town, telling the anxious families that their menfolk were safe. And some of those who had kept back the tears through all the long hours of waiting wept through sheer relief. Now they could bustle about the house and sing as they bustled, getting a hot meal ready, so that when the man got home there would be the wholesome smell of soup or broth to greet him.

And the men waiting at Lynn, still feeling the strain of that desperate struggle, were looking forward to that meal. When they got into the Midland and Great Northern Beach station they found a small crowd of friends and relatives to greet them and the warmth of that reception told a lot of the crew just how much their families had endured while they had been away.

As the branch chairman said at the annual meeting, the limelight of that year's glorious work had been focused on the service to the *Georgia*, but those who saw the boat go out on that Boxing Day and those who saw the tremendous seas crashing against the promenade sending torrents of spray, over the whole front and waited with apprehension hour after hour while the lifeboat fought its way up to the Humber, knew very well that the service excelled even the rescue work to the *Georgia*. As a test of endurance and seamanship it was the finest he could recall.

There is no system of awarding medals which is completely fair. Without belittling the awards of the Institution, this fruitless service shows that many a man who has no decorations has given noble service in life-saving endeavour. But if he may not be able to show a medal, in his heart he knows he has done his best and, as Henry Blogg said, 'That is greater than any reward.'

8

The *Monte Nevoso*

THE CROMER crew still recall with a chuckle one rough
night in 1928 when four hovellers had gone fishing off Trimingham in good weather. They were the *Admiral Jellicoe, Reaper,
Puffing Billy* and *QJJ* (Queenie, Jack, and Jimmy). Billy Davies, his
son Jimmy, and Henry Blogg were in the last-named.

The weather took a sudden change for the worse and although
the nets were quickly hauled in, they had much difficulty in
making the shore, especially as one net got around the *Reaper's*
propeller and the *Puffing Billy* broke down. The *QJJ* took them
both in tow nearly to Overstrand.

The *Admiral Jellicoe* reached Cromer first and reported the
other hovellers in difficulty. When more than an hour elapsed
with no sign of the boats the lifeboat was launched. In the mean-
time the *QJJ* had to give up her tow. By dangerous and desperate efforts the *Reaper* cleared her propeller and beached safely
at Overstrand. The *Puffing Billy* had to sail ashore there also – a
most difficult feat in the darkness and one that nearly ended in
disaster, for the boat was almost swept over a groyne with a drop
of several feet on the other side.

The *QJJ* staggered along through the gale and eventually
beached at Cromer. Henry Davies ran from the group of anxious
fishermen to meet the boat and Henry Blogg's first enquiry was,
'Where's the lifeboat gone to?'

'Gone? Why, she's gone out for you!' was the answer.

In a rare but prolonged and violent outburst Henry Blogg stormed, giving full vent to his vocabulary. He explained when he calmed down that they had seen the lights of the lifeboat in the distance and thought it had gone out on some mission. It certainly had not been near them.

The outburst of Cromer's reticent coxswain on the beach, however, was mild compared with what happened when he opened his newspaper the next morning and read the headline RESCUER RESCUED and the story of how the hero of the *Fernebo* and the *Georgia* had been saved by his own boat!

It was in February 1931 that another sudden storm caught two whelk-fishing boats at sea – the *White Heather* and *Welcome Home*, both of Sheringham. This time there was a tragic ending.

Both the Sheringham and Cromer lifeboats put out to aid the fishing-boats and while the *H. R. Upcher* of Sheringham was taking on board the crew of the *White Heather*, the *Welcome Home* tried to make the shore and was only 200 yards out when a heavy, breaking sea overwhelmed the boat. The toppling mass of water capsized and sank her, flinging the three fishermen into the water. Both lifeboats turned and headed for the spot and a fishing-boat, the *Liberty*, was launched into the tossing surf, but the engine stalled and the gallant little boat was hurled back.

The Sheringham boat manoeuvred and picked up one man while the *H. F. Bailey* headed for the other two, H. Little and John Craske. The latter was in sore distress and, although he had one arm hooked over a spar, he was apparently helpless and his head was lolling in the water. On seeing this Jack Davies the bowman kicked off his sea-boots, plunged into the icy water and swam twenty yards to John Craske and held his head up while the lifeboat hauled the other man aboard. A line was thrown to them which Jack Davies grasped and they were hauled to the *H. F. Bailey*. But as they neared the lifeboat a sea washed them both almost under her. After much struggling – for it is very difficult to get into a lifeboat from the water – they were got aboard and 'Primo' Allen applied artificial respiration. With all speed the *H.*

F. Bailey hurried back to its slipway and although the heavy seas made it most difficult to land the unconscious man, it was done and St John Ambulance men continued artificial respiration. But John Craske was dead and Jack Davies' gallantry was in vain. It was Craske's own father and brother who had launched their boat into that raging surf to aid him.

Jack Davies received a second service clasp to the Bronze Medal for his courageous effort.

The next year was a busy one for the Cromer boat and it brought one service that Henry Blogg always remembered with pleasure, for it gained him several friends; some feathered, one furred and Martin van der Hidde, the Dutch salvage officer who spent many holidays at Swallow Cottage in later years. It was to the 5000-ton *Monte Nevoso* – one of the biggest ships Henry Blogg was called to aid in peacetime and one he always spoke of affectionately afterwards as 'the good old *Monte*'.

The *Monte Nevoso* left La Plata (Buenos Aires) in October 1932 with 8600 tons of wheat, maize and linseeds, bound for Europe. Having discharged this cargo she would be homeward bound after more than eight months away from her home port Genoa and, naturally, her crew were in high spirits. Three hundred miles from Land's End her captain, Angelino Solvatore, was instructed by radio to discharge at Hull. The third officer hunted up the charts of the East Coast. The ship ran into fog when entering the Channel and proceeded at half-speed to the Forelands. In the early hours of Friday, October 14, the captain was anxiously pacing the bridge instructing his officers to try and pick up the Newarp light-vessel. He radioed his agents in Hull, giving estimated time of arrival as they were now on the last hundred miles and keeping a steady speed of nine knots. There was no sign of the guiding-light and the anxious captain was just thinking of getting a bearing from Humber radio station when an officer saw the light-vessel six miles away; just as calculated! All was well, so Captain Angelino felt he could turn in.

Then he decided to wait for the change of watch and went into the chart-room for a further study of the Haisbro' buoys.

The chief officer found him there and they pored over the charts together.

'We ought to put more to port. The flood-tide might carry us farther to starboard than we expected,' said the chief officer. Even as he spoke, from the bridge came the shout, 'Light on the port bow!'

The two officers jumped up and checked it from the port rail.

'Hard to port,' ordered the captain. Turning to his officer he cried, 'This must be the South Middle Haisbro'. These fog patches have hidden it until now. We must bring the buoy to starboard immediately.'

Hardly had he spoken when the helmsman shouted, 'The ship won't answer the helm, sir!'

The chief officer rushed to the compass. The captain signalled the engine-room 'Full speed astern'. They both swayed forward as the great propellers reversed – but the ship did not reverse! It was incredible. Without shock or sound the big ship had run on to the deadly Haisborough Sands. It was not until their own stern wave hit and lifted them farther on to the sands and dropped them heavily, that they knew beyond doubt they were well and truly stranded. It was 4 a.m. when the Italian ship struck and not until Angelino had tried without success for a long time, having got half his crew stoking to raise every pound of steam pressure to get off, did he send a message to Humber radio station asking for tug assistance. It was then 8 a.m. The ship had been four hours aground.

The coastguard at Gorleston informed Cromer of the *Monte Nevoso*'s plight and at 9.30 a.m. the *H. F. Bailey* was launched. The lifeboat reached the *Monte Nevoso* at noon and found the Dutch tug *Noordzee*, which was based on Yarmouth, already there.

The Dutch salvage officer went on board the Italian ship, seeking engagement for his tug. But Captain Angelino was not very worried as yet about his ship. He thought that when the tugs he had asked for arrived they would soon get him off the sandbank. The weather was quite calm, the sun had even broken through the clouds once or twice and there was hardly any sign of surf on the sands. It was all unfortunate but not alarming.

The *Monte Nevoso* was still trying with her own mighty engines to get free and constant soundings were taken, but they only showed the rise or fall of the tide. The ship was not buoyed! The gulls shaled and screamed monotonously around the motionless ship, as if looking for a scrap-strewn wake that was not there.

'I'm going on board,' said Henry Blogg to his second coxswain and the *H. F. Bailey* drew alongside, enabling him to climb the rope-ladder which had been let down for the tug representative.

There was a difficulty in making themselves understood, but Henry Blogg urged the Italian to accept the tug offer at once. 'The weather will soon change for the worse,' he said, lifting his cloth cap to smooth his hair forward from crown to forehead. 'We'll soon be getting a blow.'

But the captain was not impressed. He scanned the morning skies. There was to him no sign of a change and he hoped he would soon be away.

After a time the Dutch tug-man went on board again and walked amidships, looking with keen eyes for something on the decks. The Italians eyed him suspiciously, wondering what he was doing, especially when he dropped on one knee peering at the deck. Then he rose and hurried to the captain. He had found what he was looking for, a crack so small that only a trained, searching eye would have noticed it.

The captain and a couple of his officers, alarmed but still incredulous, hurried to inspect the deck over the ship's bunkers. They saw just a minute crevice in a big ship. But it was a very worried captain who rose from the deck. His ship, apparently so peacefully at rest, was being subjected to immense strain and was succumbing.

Instructing his officers to keep a watch on the crack, the captain turned to talk to the Dutchman. Henry Blogg stood looking on. He had given the Italian his opinion. He was not going to press him any more, but he knew these sands better than anyone living and he knew every moment lost went against getting the ship off. Captain Angelino engaged the tug. He would account for his action later, but he felt justified now in accepting any offer provided it was prompt. He also made Henry Blogg understand that he wanted the lifeboat to connect up the tug and to stand by during operations.

It was almost low tide and the *H. F. Bailey* coupled the *Noordzee* to the stern of the *Monte Nevoso*. The engines of the big ship, in full reverse, were given everything they would stand. The ship did not move. The five tugs the captain had asked for arrived – *Scotsman*, *Irishman*, *Hermies*, *Gelezee* and *Yorkshireman*. The lifeboat coupled them up with some difficulty, for the change Henry Blogg had forecast was now apparent. The tugs and lifeboat began bobbing with the rising swell; an ominous edge of broken water crept round the sands; the wind was getting up and the sky turning gradually darker.

The tugs had already towed two ships off the sands that week and there seemed to them a good chance of getting the *Monte Nevoso* away also. In the late afternoon the six tugs, assisted by the ship's engines, made a united attempt to break free. Again the ship did not move.

It was now getting dark, the first stars were shining like celandines and all hopes of getting off that night were abandoned. The awakened wind was whistling through the ship's rigging and the sea was beginning to get rough on the sands. As the darkness increased the lights of the *Monte Nevoso* and the tugs lit up the tumbling waters, with the smoke from funnels sweeping down through the lights. The lifeboat rode at anchor, alert and watchful, which was just as well, for three times during that night Henry Blogg had to weigh anchor and move into deeper water as the north-west gale increased.

A gale on Haisborough Sands is far worse than a gale nearer the coast. The boisterous wind pushed up the waters into heavy seas that began lifting the stern of the grounded ship and then dropping it on the sands. With a cargo of nearly 9000 tons as well as the weight of the ship, the tremendous strain can be imagined. The ship was not meant to stand that treatment. The officers watching the little gap on the deck had seen it widen appreciably and Captain Angelino was more and more troubled. The wild song of the wind in the taut wires of the rigging and the blows of the seas did not drown the groaning of the ship's structure. Then rivets began to snap with a short, sharp retort like a small-bore rifle.

When dawn spread over the grey scene the big stationary ship, the six tugs straining at the end of their ropes and the life-boat rising and falling with each sea, made a dramatic picture; like Lilliputians binding the sleeping Gulliver with their threads. It was a fight now for the life of the ship and some £60,000.

Soon there were more than the *Monte Nevoso* in difficulties, for the *Irishman* and the *Yorkshireman* broke their tows, and the *Scotsman* was so dangerously placed, being unable to keep her head to the seas, that she had to cut her tow-line. Before she did so, a wave went completely over her, leaving only mast and funnel visible. This left three tugs, and, later, the *Hermies* slipped her tow, leaving only the *Noordzee* and the *Gelezee*. There was no point in trying to reconnect the broken tows. In fact, the situation had already so deteriorated that by 6 a.m. Captain Angelino radioed 'Ship in danger'. Genoa was getting farther away.

The lifting and banging of the ship on the sands had so weakened her that long before daybreak the chief engineer said the engines must be stopped as pipes had burst and it was dangerous to work below with steam up. He feared the mighty boilers would soon be moved from their stools. So the steam, raised with such effort, was released to swirl in great clouds through the darkness and hiss louder than the howling of the gale. It meant that the *Monte Nevoso* could not help herself off the sands. The tugs must do it all.

The steam was not released any too soon, for water began entering the stokehold, followed shortly by a crash that jarred the whole ship; the boilers had broken away from their foundation, breaking all pipes and connections.

The crack amidships had grown so wide, there was now no point in measurement; the only question was, 'How long can the ship remain in one piece?'

The superintendent of the tugs had just radioed that two more tugs were on their way to the sands, but it looked as though they were going to be too late, for a mountainous sea crashed against the *Monte Nevoso* and smashed off the rudder and stern-post. The ship reeled, the great engines were dragged out of position and the engine-room became a steam-filled shambles as though hit by a torpedo. The ship was doomed. Her back was broken, her boilers, engines and rudder useless. The *Monte Nevoso* would never make her home port! There was one last violent spasm; with the crew huddled as far as they could get from the yawning gap amidships, there came a horrible rending of metal and wood as the ship was torn in two. A flood of dark-green water swirled into the hull. The crew, who twenty-four hours earlier had talked excitedly of their arrival home, now saw the imminence of great danger. They were glad of the lifeboat riding out there in deep water and the little figures now clad in oilskins and sou'westers.

At 8 a.m. Captain Angelino signalled the lifeboat, 'Please fetch us.' So Henry Blogg weighed anchor and moved in to the *Monte Nevoso*. He anchored on the weather side and veered alongside. The first few men were got into the lifeboat with the breeches-buoy, but this was such slow and dangerous work that Henry Blogg moved near enough for the crew to jump. Even so, it took an hour.

'Jump for your lives,' shouted the lifeboat-man. But it was no easy thing to jump on to a boat rising, falling and rolling with the rough sea. It was a thing that men did not practise. One of the lifeboat-men demonstrated to the *Monte Nevoso*'s crew how it should be done, for the Italians were missing many good chances when the lifeboat was almost on the crest of a wave. But still they hesitated at the critical moment.

One man missed the boat completely and fell into the sea. It seemed he must be crushed. His shipmates turned their eyes away, but Henry Blogg sheered the lifeboat and in the smother of foam the man was hooked and hauled aboard.

The seas were so heavy, the lifeboat was rising to the top of the ship's rail and then dropping twenty feet below. The seamen were encouraged to jump as the lifeboat almost reached the peak of its rise and they jostled one another waiting for the moment, then – when it came – nobody jumped. Several times the lifeboat hit the iron sides and although everything they could use as a fender was brought out, the boat was constantly damaged. Its cork fender was ripped off and everything else used as a buffer was hanging in ribbons.

When twenty-nine men and the Dutch salvage officer were transferred the captain, mate, chief engineer and wireless operator refused to leave their ship.

There was nothing more the lifeboat could do, so, with the rescued men, the *H. F. Bailey* went to Yarmouth, over twenty miles away. They arrived there at midday and the men were taken to the Mariners' Refuge. Five of the Italians had been so badly jarred in jumping that they were taken to the doctor. A fresh supply of petrol was put on the lifeboat and some of the crew who were drenched to the skin got into dry clothes. They were also ravenously hungry, having had nothing to eat except some bread and cheese since they went out twenty-seven hours earlier. Without waiting for a hot meal, which must have been a sore temptation but would have meant an hour's delay, and also declining the offer of the Great Yarmouth boat to relieve them, they put out to sea at 2 p.m. Before they left, Henry Blogg asked each member of the crew if they wished to be relieved, but they said, 'No thanks. Our job is only half done. We'll finish it.'

Henry Blogg hoped that by this time the captain would be in a different mind about leaving the ship.

They reached the wreck, but Captain Angelino was still resolved to remain.

Henry Blogg said, 'I begged the captain to leave and pointed out that he could do no good by remaining on board, but he still refused, saying, "My radio is all right. If I need assistance I will send for you".'

Once more the *H. F. Bailey* returned to Yarmouth with many a salty grumble about the obstinacy of the *Monte Nevoso*'s captain. But there, at the Mariners' Refuge, they all enjoyed their first proper meal for thirty-five hours. Before Henry Blogg went to bed he telephoned the coastguard, but there had been no message from the *Monte Nevoso*. They were near the coastguard station and close at hand should an SOS come through.

There was, however, no call, although unbeknown to them matters were desperate aboard the *Monte Nevoso*. After several hours' welcome rest the lifeboat-men turned out at 5 a.m. on Sunday morning. With two tugs, *Seaman* and *Irishman*, they returned to the wreck, reaching the sands three hours later. They found the *Monte Nevoso* in two, the funnel down and no sign of the four men.

Apparently at 9 p.m. on Saturday night, after the *Monte Nevoso's* wireless aerial had collapsed and they had taken refuge on the bridge, Captain Angelino decided it was hopeless to remain on the vessel. The four men then tried to launch one of the ship's motor-boats, first putting plenty of flares into it. It took an hour, then they cruised around in the dark, burning flares at intervals until their petrol supply had become exhausted. The boat was constantly shipping seas and uninterrupted baling was necessary. Fortunately, the weather moderated, but the exposure, first on the ship and then all night in the open boat, reduced Captain Angelino to a state of collapse. Perhaps he was also conscious that he should have listened to the advice of the men who knew these sands and this English weather.

At about 6 a.m. the Lowestoft smack *Gleam* saw red eerie flares in the distance. She had just shot her trawl, but Skipper Stone ordered the trawl to be hauled in again and he went to pick up the boat. The captain had to be assisted into the trawler and given stimulants.

The *H. F. Bailey* went alongside the deserted *Monte Nevoso* and some of the crew boarded her to be sure no one was left. While on board they heard a whimper in a cabin and on forcing the door a large dog came fawning to Henry Blogg's feet. A smaller dog was also in the cabin. The large dog was carried down a rope ladder to the lifeboat and Henry Blogg went back for the smaller animal. But when they tried to catch the terrified creature it ran away, yapping wildly and jumped over a great crack in the deck and could not be reached. In another cabin they found several cage-birds and these were also rescued.

The lifeboat scoured the sea for any sign of the ship's motor-boat, but seeing nothing the lifeboat went to the Haisbro' light-vessel to ask if conditions were suitable for berthing at Cromer. As there appeared to be a fair chance the life-boat throbbed homeward and reached the pier at 1 p.m., nearly fifty-two hours after she had been launched, having travelled seventy miles.

Henry Blogg was awarded the Silver Medal for this rescue. The Canine Defence League also awarded him its Silver Medal and the Italian Government awarded him a Silver Medal and each of the *H. F. Bailey*'s crew a Bronze Medal.

Queenie with Monte, the dog Henry Blogg and his crew had rescued from the Monte Nevoso.

The rescued dog, a Tyrolean sheepdog, was taken by the police and after six months quarantine Captain Angelino presented it to Henry Blogg. He christened it 'Monte'.

At first Henry Blogg was worried about *Monte*. When he took it to the sea the noble-looking animal would stand and bark at the water's edge and even wade into the water as though it knew that somewhere out there it had lost its master. It was feared the dog would go into the water and drown, so, for a time, whenever *Monte* came down to the sea Henry Blogg had a length of rope on its collar. Then the dog grew to love his new master and between them a deep understanding sprang up. The fisherman became deeply attached to his first and only dog. Monte died in 1935.

Some months after this rescue the postman dropped an unusual card into the letter-box at Swallow Cottage. It bore the postmark 'San Diego, California,' and read, 'At a distance of 14,000 miles we Britons have read of the splendid deed of you and your helpers. We are grateful and proud to think that we remain your fellow countrymen. Three cheers for the Island of the Sea.'

San Diego is 6000 miles from Britain across America, but the writer's window must have faced westward and he looked 14,000 miles across the Pacific, Asia and Europe to a town where Henry Blogg and other lifeboat-men were trying to teach some rescued Italian 'budgies' a few words of English.

9

The *Sepoy*

THE RNLI, having emphasised the over-riding priority of
life-saving, allows its crews to use the lifeboats for salvage
purposes also, the money thus earned being retained by them,
provided expenses such as petrol and oil are met and any damage
made good.

And when fishermen were dragging a bare living from the
sea a good salvage award could bring the sun from behind the
clouds. The lifeboat-men needed no prodding on a salvage job.
This was especially true when they were vying with tugmen, for
rivalry was often keen and epithets flew from boat to tug like
driven spume.

Henry Blogg was an artist in salvage. His every move was
purposeful, crisply efficient and pleasing to watch. There was no
indecision or bungling when he was trying to get a good ship
out of the snare of the sands. But in a court-room, when his sal-
vage-cases were being tried, he was miserable and ill at ease, for
he loathed the witness box. He appeared more comfortable in
a North Sea blizzard on Haisborough Sands than in a centrally
heated court of law.

The Cromer coxswain tackled salvage-work not only from a
business angle but also because he hated the loss of a good ship.
It did not matter if he had never seen the vessel before or whether
it was British or Chinese. The fact that it was a ship was sufficient

to give him a sense of personal loss if it was destroyed. When he saw a vessel needlessly lost through bad seamanship or salvage-work, especially in wartime, he was indignant as well as sad-dened. By his own initiative and energy he saved many ships that would otherwise have become total wrecks.

One example will show how smart the lifeboat-men could be at this game.

A trawler went aground on the east side of the Haisborough Sands. A strong east wind was blowing and a heavy swell running. Two tugs were towing in tandem and straining their 'innards' against wind and sea when the trawler suddenly refloated. With feminine contrariness, however, she decided she would go with the sea and not with the tugs. This lack of har-mony broke the tow. The tugs lurched forward with the sudden release, burying their noses in the seas and the trawler began bumping and knocking over the sands, right across to the west side. There, as if completely exhausted, she stuck fast. Henry Blogg in the lifeboat accompanied the runaway over the sands and as soon as she stuck again he immediately ran alongside, passed a tow to the vessel and, pulling with the wind and sea, got the ship into deep water long before the two tugs could get round the north end of the sands to join them. The chagrin of the tug-men can be imagined.

That was a business proposition executed in a businesslike way. When it was a matter of saving life things were different. If the lifeboat-men weighed the monetary reward against the risk and the hardships they would not save many lives. Henry Blogg was chiefly impelled by the motive of mercy in his work. This great seaman was undoubtedly moved by compassion to the heights of courage and sacrifice and he inspired his men to climb with him. But the nearest he ever got to admitting this was a year or so before the rescue of the *Sepoy*. A crab-boat capsized off the beach and a friend of Henry Blogg who was not a fisher-man helped to get another boat off to the rescue. He pushed and heaved as far as the water's edge and then stopped. The boat was launched and the men were saved.

Henry Blogg kept the incident brewing in his mind for many days, then one evening he came round to it.

'They tell me you didn't help to launch the boat when they went after those men last week,' he said.

'Yes, I did,' said his friend, 'but I didn't go into the water.'

'Why not?'

'Well, I was at work and didn't want to get my shoes and trousers wet.'

'Oh! Well, supposing that it had been me out there in the water, what would you have done?'

'I should have gone right in, but that's different, you're my friend.'

'That won't do,' said Henry Blogg. 'Suppose when I got a call I said, "I'm not going out to them chaps. They're strangers to me," the lifeboat would never go out. When I go out I don't know who they are. I don't even know whether they're English. I go because they need me. Now, don't let it happen again.'

And Henry Blogg' s friend said later, 'I saw, then, how wrong I had been.'

The power of mercy as a motive was never more clearly shown than in the rescue of the *Sepoy* at Cromer in 1933. That service was undoubtedly one of the most thrilling in the history of the sea. As Sir Godfrey Baring, Chairman of the RNLI, said: 'No more splendid example of courage, resolution and brilliantly skilful seamanship has ever been displayed round our coasts.'

It took place just off the beach at Cromer where hundreds of holidaymakers had sported on the sand and where the *Fernebo* had run aground sixteen years before. A score of dramatic photographs were taken and pictures went round the world. People who had never been to Cromer saw and remembered the *Sepoy*.

On December 13, 1933, a bitterly cold easterly gale suddenly sprang up and whipped across England, bringing a real taste of Arctic conditions. The east coast naturally caught the full brunt of the gale; and gusts of sixty-two miles an hour were registered off Yarmouth. Not only was Cromer caught in the icy grip of Siberian winds, but towering seas lashed the coast, so that east coast lifeboats were in tragic demand. Seven boats were launched during the morning and early afternoon of that wild day: Blakeney, Sheringham, Great Yarmouth and Gorleston and both Cromer boats from Norfolk; the Aldeburgh boat from Suffolk and the Bridlington boat from Yorkshire.

In spite of magnificent courage and seamanship, that freezing gale took grievous toll of life and ships. The SS *Culmore* of Londonderry with nine men foundered off Aldeburgh before the lifeboat could reach her. She left not a spar or piece of wreckage. The *Broomfleet* of Goole left the Humber with a crew of thirteen, bound for Ipswich, but never made the Suffolk port. No trace of her was ever found. What happened no one knows, but the bodies of some of her crew were cast up on the Norfolk coast.

Heavy as was the loss of life, it would have been far heavier but for the lifeboats.

It was 4 a.m. when Cromer got the first call for help. 4 a.m.! What a test for morale and manhood, to answer the call of the maroons at that hour, with the bleak onshore wind howling like a demon!

Henry Blogg had slept none too well and between dozes he had heard the wind increasing and knew it was from the danger quarter. He felt it was just the sort of night he would be needed.

Out in the mad turmoil of waters a barge, the *Glenway*, had got into difficulties and even as the Cromer coxswain turned restlessly in bed the three men on board had struggled feverishly to save their ship. The wind and the surge of dark waters pushed them remorselessly towards the shore. There were no rocks awaiting them on the soft Norfolk coastline, but more ships had died in these waters than on any rocky coast. Realising they were powerless to stop that drift on to the lee shore, they burned distress flares and – though the night was murky as an Egyptian tomb – the watchful Happisburgh coastguard saw the faint distant glow, waited to be sure it was not an illusion, then, when it was repeated, noted the direction and telephoned Cromer that the flares seemed perilously close inshore.

When Henry Blogg picked up the receiver he was instantly

alert and expectant. The wind was rattling fiercely the landing-window and some corrugated iron sheets had blown loose and were banging in a yard nearby. Tersely he was told of flares eleven miles down the coast off Happisburgh. 'Bang away,' said Blogg, accepting the responsibility for the launch. And while the coastguard ran into the night to fire the maroons, Blogg was calling the mechanic William Davies. He then scrambled into his clothes and was dragging on his sea-boots as the first signal boomed over the sea. The dull sound stirred Cromer. Its towns-folk who had no need to respond turned over in their beds, sparing a thought for the 'poor devils out there,' and for their own men who had to answer that call on such a night.

Henry Blogg, having told Ann what the call was about, was soon out of the house and running down Corner Street, flashing his torch as he went. Billy Davies had beaten him to the boat-house and as the coxswain clumped along the hollow-sounding planks of the pier, leaning forward against the gale, he saw the lights appear in the windows of the lifeboat-house. The search-light above the slipway stabbed the night. He had not reached the end of the 550-foot pier before another man had dashed through the iron entrance-gates and behind him, like dancing stars, shone the lights of other men descending the cliff gangways.

Inside the boat-house the wind battered the folding doors and seemed to shake the wooden sides of the house, while from underneath sounded the deep booming of waves striking and sucking round the pier-supports. Henry Blogg got his oilskins and belt and saw the coastguard enter and make for the doors to open them. Billy Davies was already starting the winch-engine.

The boat-house was filled with activity and noise as the engines roared into life and the rest of the crew arrived, scrambled into their gear and climbed into the big blue-and-white boat. Henry Blogg noted all present and heard the coastguard shout that the bow-chain was away and saw him standing ready to release the stern-pin.

All set! The coxswain yelled the order and, with a sharp blow, the quick-release pin was knocked out. As though reluctant to take the cold plunge, the *H. F. Bailey* hovered, then moved and began to slide with increasing speed out of the boat-house and down the slipway into the angry sea that was already rushing half-way up to meet it. The slipway light showed the waves whipped to white fury as far as the eye could reach.

In a smother of spray the boat hit the sea and Henry Blogg gripped the wheel firmly for his 160th launch, the engines racing at 'Full speed ahead'.

For two hours the *H. F. Bailey* fought the gale and towering seas down the coast to Happisburgh. There, before dawn had lightened the scene, they found the spritsail barge *Glenway* with two men and a boy on her. Despite all the crew's efforts, the barge had been driven ashore near Cart Gap. She lay in shallow water with a deadly surf bursting about her, so that the lifeboat could not go alongside. Twice they tried to get closer to take the men off, but at the last attempt the lifeboat itself grounded and all the crew had to haul and push with boat-hooks to get her off. Henry Blogg decided to stand by until the tide had ebbed sufficiently to leave the *Glenway* high enough on the beach for the crew to get safely ashore.

So they waited, watching the gale whipping up the beach-sand like a desert sandstorm. The cold was even more intense. That east wind would have penetrated armour-plate. As there was no hope of getting rehoused at Cromer and it was nearly 8 a.m., Henry Blogg decided to carry on to Gorleston. It was seventeen miles – a long journey in those exceptional seas – and wave after wave hit them, sweeping over the boat. They were 'taking it green' time and again. The cold and their drenched clothes made every man long for the shelter of the harbour.

As they passed Palling coastguard station Henry Blogg signalled to ask if there was any other call for them at Cromer, as he felt they might be wanted at home. Visibility, however, was so bad that the signals could not be read and they carried on to the Cockle Gat and between the shoals and sandbanks of the Yarmouth Roads.

Henry Blogg's forethought in signalling Palling was typical of his leadership and judgement. It was justified; even before they left the *Glenway* a similar disaster had happened at Cromer.

This time it was the sixty-five-ton *Sepoy*, of Dover, another barge with two men aboard. The *Sepoy* had anchored two miles east of Cromer pier to ride out the worst of the gale. The coastguard had kept a fatherly eye on her and had seen her anchor-light clearly several times. He had seen no distress flares, although Captain Joseph Hemstead stated later he had burnt two. The *Sepoy* was not happy, however, for the fierceness of the gale and enormous seas rolling in with the weight of the troubled North Sea behind them made both her anchors drag and she moved with irresistible forces behind her towards the shore. The captain and his mate, a young man of twenty, worked like fury to stop the fatal drift, but with them, as with the *Glenway*, nothing availed. The storm had the mastery. They hoisted a distress signal and hoped and prayed the anchors might suddenly bite.

From a position almost opposite Overstrand the barge moved nearer and nearer to the shore and to Cromer. The coastguard and a rapidly swelling crowd saw the helpless ship being driven inshore. F. H. Barclay, fearing the *H. F. Bailey*, with both coxswain and second coxswain on her, might be some time before she returned, asked Robert Davies to take out the reserve boat *Alexandra*. In addition, the life-saving apparatus was quickly brought up opposite the spot where the *Sepoy*, in a rush of foam and with a sickening lurch, had grounded.

Robert Davies was well over sixty. He had been one of the best mechanics in the lifeboat service, but failing sight had compelled him to retire much against his wish. A scratch crew of lifeboat-men, fishermen and members of the Rocket Brigade was got together. Henry Davies, then eighteen, was the youngest member, the next oldest was forty-two and all the others were between fifty and sixty-five. One lad of fourteen, Frank Davies, got a belt and was preparing to go, but his brother Henry would not let him.

What this emergency crew lacked in experience they made up for in enthusiasm. The No. 1 boat was away and here was a job to

The Sepoy *in difficulties: off the east beach at Cromer as one of the unsuccessful rocket lines is fired.*

be done. They would prove their mettle to the 'regulars'.

There was no shortage of volunteer launchers either. At least a hundred were ready at the old boat-house – women among them – to launch the *Alexandra* and her crew of twelve. Tom 'Bussey' Allen was rushing about organising the launchers. Even the inexperienced could see it would be a heartbreaking struggle to get the boat away through that murderous surf.

Down the slope and over the sands they pushed and pulled the lifeboat. The leading launchers were waist-deep in the icy sea before they got her off with a rush and a rousing cheer into the seething foam. But no sooner had her oarsmen begun to pull than a rearing mass of water hit her and washed her back, flinging her broadside on the beach, with her crew spilling into the surf. There is no trifling with the sea at Cromer when an easterly gale is blowing.

Disappointed but not dismayed, they heaved and tugged and got the heavy boat on to skeats and then back on her carriage and again they launched her. The oars struck in unison immediately she was afloat and that scratch crew pulled with might and main against the insweeping breakers. For twenty minutes, swearing, pulling, panting, gaining a little, losing a little, they struggled with magnificent determination. The sight of those two desperate men on the *Sepoy*, so near and yet so far from land, egged them on. But no power of arm or skill with the oar could make any appreciable headway. Once more the *Alexandra* was tossed back, almost contemptuously, on the beach.

While this struggle was going on the barge drifted even nearer the shore, bumping on the bottom, with the hissing, seething waters running and spilling at will over her hull, so that the crew had to take to the rigging. The spray, flung high with each bursting breaker, reached up as though to drag them from their temporary refuge. Finally the Sepoy came to rest at the bottom of the 'Doctor's Steps' where the *Fernebo* had rested long ago and where Henry Blogg had his beach-tent hiring-hut. The tide came in very high, reaching at its highest point the bottom of the east gangway.

But neither launchers nor crew would admit defeat – the prize was so near. Again they heaved the boat on to the carriage and, changing their tactics, dragged it over the rough beach for half a mile, a hundred willing helpers hauling at ropes and pushing the shafts. Tom Allen was magnificent in encouraging his big team. Swearing and laughing in drenched clothes, he urged and instructed. The plan was to get to windward and sufficiently out to sea to veer down on the *Sepoy*.

They also double-banked some of the oars with fishermen from Runton and Overstrand who had gathered there. Tom Allen was swept headlong from the carriage by a wave, but this time the *Alexandra* was successfully launched.

Meanwhile, Cromer had abandoned its usual routine – meals and work were forgotten. Folk were drawn to the shore as by a magnet – the magnet of heroism – to see another great rescue-

The No 2 lifeboat Alexandra *makes one of its unsuccessful attempts to reach the* Sepoy. *Henry 'Shrimp' Davies, who was to follow Henry Blogg as Cromer's cox'n, rowed port bow oar.*

drama. Many there remembered every detail of the *Fernebo* epic and they compared the determination of this crew of elderly men with the aged crew of 1917. From a score of vantage points along the cliff they looked out over the sea whipped white by the wind. They saw their reserve boat struggle gallantly to get away from the broken water and with mounting tension watched it gain foot by foot, drawing slowly away from the beach and then edging towards the *Sepoy*. They were going to do it! The spectators encouraged them with burst after burst of cheering, but for all the 'routing' and their heart-bursting efforts they could not master those great waves. The seas carried them between the shore and the wreck, defeating their purpose. It had also thwarted another attempt, for while they had been battling the line-throwing guns had been in action. Four lines had been fired and the last had fallen right across the stern of the *Sepoy*. The barge rolled with each sea, but the young mate had climbed down from the rigging and, gauging his opportunity, had crowded over the flooded fore-deck and grabbed the line. Then he started to get back, but a wave washed completely over him. Fortunately he had flung himself flat, grabbed the rail and hung on for life while the water spent itself. The captain came down to help and together they got the line into the rigging.

But Fate was not being kind for, even as they dragged the rope with them, the struggling lifeboat was swept past by the force of the sea and fouled the line that might have saved them. The rope parted. A groan replaced the cheers on the lips of thousands of watchers. It was obvious that the pounding of the barge would soon break it up, as the tide was running higher. The *Alexandra* had narrowly averted disaster herself as she was carried past the wreck, for the waves took her right over the breakwater, which might have ripped the bottom out of her. For the third and last time she was flung on to the beach, near her own boat-house.

The two desperate men in the rigging climbed higher while the pathetic distress-signal streamed in the gale and the shreds of their sails flapped and swirled, as though echoing their own alarm. The hatchway had been burst open and the hold flooded. The ship was bucking like a bronco, with two half-frozen men trying to keep their insecure perch.

All efforts had failed – the questions now on a thousand lips were: `Where's the Bailey? Where's Blogg?'

Nobody knew. Since 10 a.m. the coastguard had been trying to contact the No. 1 boat in vain, but it was thought they would head for Gorleston, being unable to get back to their own slip-way. So Gorleston were told of the *Sepoy*'s plight. When the message was received, to save precious time they at once launched their own boat to meet and warn Henry Blogg. The two lifeboats met eight miles from Gorleston, not far from the Cockle light-vessel. That prompt action had saved the *H. F. Bailey* sixteen miles!

Henry Blogg was not surprised at the message, although he growled in anxious annoyance to think they had come all this way south when they were needed on their own doorstep. It was nearly twenty miles back, in the teeth of a fierce freezing wind.

Henry Blogg said afterwards, 'The journey up and down was the worst in my twenty-four-years' experience as coxswain. It took us two hours to get to Happisburgh.' Coxswain Fleming, of the Great Yarmouth boat, said the seas were as bad as he had ever experienced. Second coxswain Hutchinson, of Bridlington, said he had not been in such a gale for years. The Sheringham boat double-banked all oars but could not get alongside a grounded barge. The sea was stronger than all their efforts.

With the terrible sense of urgency oppressing the Cromer men they made the best speed they could, fearing they might be too late. In view of the extreme cold and the grim task ahead, Henry Blogg took what was for him a most unusual course by opening the emergency ration cupboard and issuing a tot of rum to his men although he took none himself.

For three hours and a half they battled northward against seas that continually tried to snatch overboard the entire crew. Then, on the cliff-tops at Cromer, the people saw a small black object in the grey distance and as it grew in size someone suddenly recognised it as the lifeboat. A cheer arose and ran along the whole front. Even the most stolid and restrained watchers took up the cry, 'The *Bailey*'s coming. Blogg is here!' To have stood in that crowd and felt that surge of hope was a great testimony to Cromer's coxswain. It was as though the men were already rescued. Such was the confidence in his prowess.

Captain Hemstead and John Stevenson of Grays, Essex, clinging with numb hands to icy ropes, heard the cheer. It brought new strength to them, although they could see nothing. They had nearly given up the struggle to live and were almost past feeling or caring, so numb were their bodies and brains from exposure.

The incoming tide had put 200 yards of churned, seething water between the *Sepoy* and the shore. The thunderous roar of breakers and moving shingle made speech difficult. The seas came riding proudly in, one behind another, with ragged foaming crests and the wind whipping their heads into white smoke. The sea-wall was pounded by savage billows that smashed against the concrete, then broke in a welter of spray and spume.

The lifeboat H. F. Bailey *as Henry Blogg drives her onto the deck of the* Sepoy *and the* Sepoy's *crew are helped from the rigging.*

The breakers were racing over the *Sepoy*, tearing her to pieces.

As the *H. F. Bailey* approached Henry Blogg took in the situation and realised his best plan would be to anchor to windward and drop down to the barge, as the *Alexandra* had tried to do in her final attempt. But, on getting closer, he saw that was impossible, for the *Sepoy*'s anchors and other cables fouled that approach. It also looked well-nigh hopeless to get to the lee side of the ship and get alongside, but perhaps there was just a chance and anyway, it must be tried. The biggest danger would be that a wave might catch them when they turned broadside to get alongside the *Sepoy*.

Knowing how great was the risk he was taking, Henry Blogg judged his distance, anxiously watching the breakers, spun the wheel and gave two quick orders to get between the barge and the shore. Every man was taut at his post, but the force of water was more powerful than their fine engine and they were swept past the wreck. Once more this great seaman brought the boat round and repeated the manoeuvre. It failed. It was not going to work. The odds were too heavily against them. The shipwrecked men watched with rising and falling hopes and the great crowd first yelled and then fell silent. Photographers took hurried photographs.

Henry Blogg brought the helm round again. His face and oil-skins streamed with salt water, but he was alert and determined in spite of the great strain he had already undergone since 3 a.m. that morning. He could see the *Alexandra* on the beach and guessed she had tried her utmost. He must save these men if it was humanly possible, but on no account must these wild seas catch his boat as they had caught the Caister boat and tipped it over, like a basin in the surf.

The third attempt was beaten by the power of wind and wave, but they did get close enough for the bowman to throw and secure a grapnel. Jack Davies stood in the bows making a symbolic picture Captain Hemstead never forgot. The hook flew through the air and caught in the rigging of the barge. In a flash it was fast to a bollard and the lifeboat was held. Rescue was now possible. But the seas had not finished. Even as the tautened rope checked the lifeboat and another line was being thrown, a mountain of green water with foaming crest seized the *H. F. Bailey* and smashed it into the *Sepoy*. The lifeboat was holed and the grapnel line broken, but it might have been worse – much worse!

The failure and near-disaster determined Henry Blogg on his next course. He had tried orthodox methods and three times they had failed. The men in the rigging had been exposed to icy water and wind for eight hours. They were nearly at the end of their endurance. Something must be done, even if it was drastic and risky, so the coxswain, forsaking the text-book of seamanship, yelled an order to two or three of the crew and the mechanics to hold fast and be ready for quick action. He swung his boat, circled the *Sepoy* and then from the lee side pointed the bows at the barge and – with a quick order to his mechanic – drove straight

With the crew of the Sepoy *safely on board, the* H. F. Bailey *backs away from the grounded vessel before turning and beaching.*

at the wreck and right on top of the barge, close to the rigging where the men were hanging. The *H. F. Bailey's* bows rose on a wave and bore down on the bulwarks of the *Sepoy,* smashing them, and holding the boat for a few moments. In the shattering jar of that crash the lifeboat-men were almost jolted from their hold, then three of them reached over the gunwale and dragged the young mate, who seemed unconscious and unable to leave the rigging, into the lifeboat. They were just turning back for Captain Hemstead when a sea lifted the lifeboat and swept her off the *Sepoy.*

Henry Blogg swore in disappointment and anxiety. He did not want to repeat that dangerous operation but there was no choice. He shouted that he was going in again and watching his moment, repeated the bold manoeuvre. For a second time, by brilliant seamanship, he drove his boat into almost the same spot on the wreck and in that brief check his men helped Captain Hemstead, his money still safe about his person, from the barge to the *H. F. Bailey*. The sea herself, as if tired of the struggle and admitting her defeat, lifted the boat clear of the deck and away from the menacing cables.

The stem of the lifeboat had been broken off and a couple of holes had been knocked in the sides through which the sea poured into the compartments behind. But the men were saved!

It was not yet all over, however, although the crowd yelled themselves hoarse in admiration of that brilliant rescue. The cox-swain had another vital decision to make. He could not get back to the slipway in those seas and he was short of fuel. If he ran down the coast again to Gorleston, twenty-eight miles or four hours away, it might cost the lives of the two rescued men. They were both in very poor shape and four hours' delay would prob-ably be fatal. Moreover, his own crew were all-in after twelve hours, in which they had been soaked through from the moment of launching and were chilled to the marrow. No, it could not be the slipway and it must not be Gorleston, but there was one other way left – a most dangerous way. Henry Blogg brought the bows of the *H. F. Bailey* to point at a sandy spot on the beach and then, in dread lest a surprise wave might capsize them, with briefly opened throttle he 'rallied' to the shore. With a grinding jolt the lifeboat beached and even as they did so Tom 'Bussey' Allen (who had already had to change three times that day) and a dozen men ran out into the icy sea to steady the *H. F. Bailey* with ropes. Others hastened to help the *Sepoy*'s men out of the lifeboat and ashore. The young rescued man was placed on a stretcher and taken to hospital for treatment while the captain was assisted to the Red Lion Hotel.

Of the great crowd of watchers, many caught cold and some developed pneumonia after that long wait in the bitter wind. Tom 'Bussey' said his father became very ill and one old person died from a chill. But they cheered their crew and coxswain to the echo. And suddenly from the lofty tower of the church came a crash of bells that pealed in joy and pride for the Cromer crews.

They crowded around Henry Blogg, cheering and acclaiming him. Then he was told of Robert Davies' efforts with the emergency crew. With salt caking on his red face and hands, Henry Blogg listened intently. His eyes were bloodshot with sea-water and he looked utterly exhausted, but he said, 'That's one of the finest things I've heard of.' He added that his own crew had been 'magnificent', and made his way through the crowd home to Swallow Cottage.

The next morning the national press carried banner headlines and magnificent pictures of the rescue. Millions read of Henry Blogg's latest exploit – 'nobility of purpose – heroism – seamanship – daring – sacrifice' – all the qualities that the croakers had said modern Britain had lost. A nation with the greatest sea traditions in history felt very proud of its lifeboat-men.

It took twenty hours' continuous hard work with blocks and

With a calm sea and low tide, the wreck of the Sepoy *could be visited and the damage seen.*

jacks to get the damaged *H. F. Bailey* afloat. Then, on a calm sea, she was taken to Lowestoft for repairs and was ready a week later for service.

For this rescue Henry Blogg, now aged fifty-eight, received a second service clasp to his Silver Medal and the crew received the thanks of the Institution on vellum, as did gallant Robert Davies.

On the beach the broken *Sepoy* was a source of interest for many days. Visitors walked around her at low tide. They stared at her cargo of tiles spilled all about the battered hull. The mast with its bedraggled sail and broken rigging still stood, the centre of one of the greatest dramas enacted on that wreck-strewn coast. When the sea had pounded most of the barge to driftwood, on the bows in dirty white lettering one could still read: SEPOY. Today that name brings back to Cromer's lifeboat-men memories of one of their worst hammerings. Tom 'Bussey' summed it up in Norfolk dialect, 'Du I remember the *Sepoy*? Ah, bor, thet wus a troshin'!'

So it was, but the name is also coupled with what secretary Barclay described in his report of the rescue: 'A wonderful exhibition of coxswain Blogg's splendid and faultless seamanship.'

10

Endurance

CHARLIE COX was the 'strong man' of the Cromer crew. He was thickset and as powerful as an ox.

Whenever a boat got stuck on the beach and no efforts of her crew would move her, the cry would go up, 'Charlie! Where's Charlie?' And Charlie Cox would arrive, put his enormous shoulders to the boat and the job was done. But for all his strength he was a gentle, kind-hearted man and Henry Blogg had a great affection for him. He was dependable and – above all – would do a job that needed doing without being told. Henry Blogg liked that. One day, however, Charlie used his initiative to try and fool his skipper. He failed, for a man had to get up very early to take in Henry Blogg on matters pertaining to the sea.

It happened this way.

Henry Murrell did a spot of fishing from Cromer pier when on holiday. It amused him and did not deplete the North Sea appreciably. In fact, Henry Blogg was always chipping his lawyer about his lack of success and seeing him baiting his hooks one day he remarked, 'Wasting your time again, Murrell?'

The solicitor was game. 'Henry,' he said, 'I'm going to get you a really nice sole for your tea.'

'H'm,' grunted Henry Blogg, in an I'll-believe-it-when-I-see-it tone and walked away.

Henry Murrell did not really fancy his chances and he hurried to find Charlie Cox. 'Charlie,' he said, 'I'm in a fix. I've promised Henry a sole for his tea. What can you do about it?'

Charlie did not know but promised to help and later that morning the big fisherman turned up with a magnificent sole he had netted near the beach. Henry Murrell put a hook in its mouth and tore it out, wrapped the fish in grease-proof paper and took it to Swallow Cottage. Henry Blogg was not at home, so he gave it to Ann, saying, 'I promised Henry this for his tea. He knows all about it.'

The next day Henry Blogg saw him on the beach and before the amateur fisherman could open his mouth the professional said firmly,

'You didn't catch that off the pier, Murrell!'

'Did you enjoy it, Henry? I like to keep my promise.'

'You didn't catch it off the pier.'

'It was a nice sole, wasn't it, Henry?'

'It was a very nice sole, but you didn't catch it off the pier.'

So it went on for two more days. Charlie Cox was kept informed and sworn to secrecy. Each time the two Henrys met the subject came up and Blogg ended with 'You didn't catch it off the pier.'

On the day the solicitor's holiday ended Henry Blogg said to him, 'That sole was caught in a net off the beach, Murrell, wasn't it?'

Henry Murrell knew the game was up. 'How did you know?' he asked.

'Because there was a little weed on it that you find near the beach but not out in deep water!' came the answer.

Henry Blogg was well schooled in his work and in addition, although his schooling at a desk had been short, his handwriting and his English were good. The hawk-eyed seaman could write an interesting letter. His incoming mail too was always interesting, especially after a big rescue.

Letters arrived from all parts of the world and his wife spent hours reading and re-reading them. Sometimes gifts of money were sent for the Institution or the Cromer crew and sometimes it was a gift for the coxswain, as in 1934 when he was presented with a valuable and historic pipe. The accompanying letter told how it had been presented to the donor's great-great-uncle, a vice-admiral, by George III in recognition of victories over the French.

In 1794 the vice-admiral was having a cannon-ball and grape-shot battle with the *Sybille*. He drove the Frenchman ashore and then, with commendable chivalry, hoisted a flag of truce, hauled the stranded foe off the shore and re-started the fight.

'The vice admiral,' said the donor, 'was a great sailor and made his name by killing Frenchmen. His pipe now passes to a much greater seaman, whose name will survive much longer for saving men of all races.'

Henry Blogg never smoked it but he thought a lot of it. Like many other non-smokers, the coxswain had a sweet tooth, with a particular failing for chocolates. He was also a fruit-eater and if he never preached the doctrine that 'an apple a day keeps the doctor away,' he practised it.

Henry Blogg could be stubborn and exasperating, but never petty-minded. He was a big man, big enough to give without wanting the credit for giving. Many times on Christmas Eve he would be talking in Jackson's butcher's shop and, seeing a fisherman pass who he knew was feeling the pinch of difficult times, he would call him in.

'What have you got for tomorrow, Jack?'

'Nothing as yet Henry.'

'Well, you'd better pick something here and I'll make it right.'

The fisherman would pick a fowl or a joint and the coxswain would pay, adding, 'You needn't talk about it.'

Jimmy Dumble, ex-coxswain of the Sheringham boat, speaking of his fairness, said, 'Henry was a good payer.'

When asked what he meant, he replied, 'Well, Cromer once got a call to a salvage job, but several of our men went off to help in their boats. In fact, there were more of us than from Cromer, but Henry let us in on the job. Mind you, he needn't have done. Afterwards, when I suggested that we should go fifty-fifty, Henry insisted that we should share man for man. That was more than fair dealing.'

The year 1935 was one of grievous loss for Henry Blogg. His dog Monte died; his fine boat, the *H. F. Bailey*, which he had commanded since 1924 and to which he and his crew had become much attached, was replaced by a new one, the *H. F. Bailey III*; his friend F. H. Barclay, who had been honorary secretary since 1908, died; and his beloved daughter Queenie also died in Cromer hospital after a perplexing and distressing illness.

Queenie had always been frail and since leaving a private school had assisted in the house and, during the season, with the beach business. She did all the booking and correspondence of the firm and wrote capable, business-like letters. Being delicate, always at home and the only daughter, the blow was the greater. There had been a deep bond of understanding between the strong man and the frail girl and her death while still in her twenties cast a pall of grief over Henry and Ann. It was as though both fire and light had gone out and they sat alone in a chilly, dark room.

Henry Blogg hardly spoke to anyone for months. He seemed a heartbroken man and shut himself up with his sorrow.

Long after, on being asked by some people who did not know him, 'Have you any children?' he paused a long time and they thought

Queenie in happier days on the tennis courts.

he was not going to answer; then he said, 'I had a daughter . . . once . . . but the doctors could not save her. . . . Life is not worth living any more!'

When his friend Alec Jackson ventured a word of comfort he said, 'I shall have to get over it, Jackie, but in my own way.'

On the few occasions Henry Blogg got really riled his language could be as sulphurous as any fisherman's on the beach, but after Queenie's death he never swore again.

Those who knew him best hesitated before even mentioning her name to him although, eventually, he would talk to those nearest to him about her. But the wound never healed.

Henry Blogg had to take on the booking and writing his daughter had so efficiently done and it came very hard to him. He was more used to a helm than a pen. As he tried to pick up the threads so suddenly snapped he came across things Queenie had said or written to customers and little kindnesses she had done for them and the big, rough hand brushed away a tear before he could continue.

It was the year after Queenie's death that Henry Blogg showed how at sixty his amazing powers of endurance were undiminished.

Although as a boy he had been spindly, an easy prey for bullies and had taken no part in games, in manhood he displayed great powers of endurance and retained them into advanced years. There was the remarkable instance of the SS *Inverawe* in December 1920, when the lifeboat stood by the grounded ship assisting tugs from midday on Sunday until midday on the following Thursday, provisions being brought out to her by a crabboat. There was also a forty-three-hour service to the SS *Zembra* in November 1932. But, from a score of examples, the most striking was given in November 1936 during a four-day period of severe gales. There were seven launches during that time at Cromer and Yarmouth. The first came at 11 a.m. on November 16 when the Haisbro' light-vessel reported a steamer aground on the sands three miles south-east by east of her.

The *H. F. Bailey* achieved one of her best launching times, being afloat within ten minutes of receiving this report.

An hour and a half later they found the 1800-ton *Nesttun*, of Tvedestrand, in the position given. She carried a crew of sixteen and was making for London, having crossed the North Sea from Trondheim with a cargo of wood-pulp.

A moderate west-north-west breeze was blowing and the sea was whipped white on the sands when Henry Blogg arrived, but he thought there was an excellent chance of getting the ship refloated. He therefore went aboard and offered to assist in getting her off. The captain accepted and radioed for two tugs. The lifeboat stood by until these arrived and then connected them to the Nesttun.

The tugs made two gallant attempts, straining with every ounce of power at their tow-lines in the heavy seas, their sterns almost under water, and the *Nesttun* put her own engines at 'full astern'; but it all made no difference. She seemed glued to the sands. It was evident more tug power was needed before she would shift, so a call was made for another two tugs. After a long wait, while the dark clouds rolled overhead as if to meet the approaching night, the tugs arrived and the *H. F. Bailey* carried their tow-lines with much difficulty and danger to the Norwegian ship. No further attempt could be made owing to darkness and the rough seas, so the lifeboat stood by throughout a very blustering night. While the townsfolk of Cromer slept in their warm beds their lifeboat crew spent a sleepless, uncomfortable night riding a stormy sea and waiting for the dawn.

The new day brought little improvement in the weather, but a united attempt was made with the four tugs and the *Nesttun*'s engines. Again they failed. The sands held the ship like a vice. The only thing to do was to lighten the vessel, so for most of that day as many men as could be mustered heaved the deck-cargo overboard. Thousands of pounds' worth of goods were flung as a sacrifice on to the sands. In the late afternoon the tugs, harnessed like a four-horse Greek chariot, tried once more and this time with the help of a racing flood-tide – although hampered by darkness – they moved the ship. It was only a yard at first, then, gradually, with the lift of the water, the pull of the towlines and the threshing of her own propellers she came clear of the sands. The *Nesttun* had been saved and the Haisborough Sands cheated of a victim.

The lifeboat had done her work and it was time to get home to

Henry Blogg in a portrait from his younger days. As with the later portrait on page 51, it is thought this picture may be by Olive Edis.

a change of clothes and a hot meal. A man can grow very tired of salt water, high winds, a small boat and a dreary seascape with an all-encircling horizon after twenty or thirty hours.

On the return journey, while off Mundesley, Henry Blogg tried to contact the coastguard by radio to enquire about conditions at Cromer, but he could not do so. The lifeboat went on to Cromer, arriving at midnight. Lights were still twinkling from the dark, mounded outline of the town, for a dance was in progress. Then the lights came on in the boat-house, but the weather was too bad to re-house. The coxswain decided to wait for low water.

For over two hours the tired men rode the seas off the pier-head, watching the lights gradually go out. Young women in dance-frocks drew their wraps around them and hurried home through the wind-swept streets. The drenched lifeboat-men shivered as the wind grew colder and rougher. Further waiting was now useless, for the weather was worsening. Moreover, petrol was getting uncomfortably low in the tanks, so Henry Blogg thought it best to go to Wells, which was the nearest port. They set off in a north-west direction, but in half an hour the wind increased to gale force and they were running full into it, plunging into big seas and taking water continually. In these conditions they would not be able to get into Wells harbour and the only course left was to turn round and run before the wind to Gorleston.

Their plight was now serious. They had forty miles to go and fuel was running low. If the engine did stall in those seas it would be disastrous.

Running at half speed to save petrol, they throbbed down the coast through the early-morning darkness with the gale helping them. They had picked out the Cockle buoys and then – just before daybreak – saw a vessel apparently high on the beach where no boat could approach her. Owing to their own fuel-shortage they dare not investigate more fully by waiting for daylight, but carried on to Gorleston and reported what they had seen. They arrived at 8 a.m. with only three gallons of petrol in the tank, having been at sea for forty-five hours. Many of the crew had been wet through nearly all the time.

The lifeboat moored at the quay near the Gorleston lifeboat-house and the rough-chinned, haggard-eyed coxswain and crew went back to Cromer by road for dry clothes and rest.

The coxswain of a lifeboat, however, is like a one-man business – he can leave the premises but not the responsibility. There was an appetising smell as Henry Blogg opened the front-door of Swallow Cottage, for Ann had prepared a meal after having been warned by telephone. Henry Blogg had a change of clothes and a change from standing for hours at the wheel of the boat. But he did not have much rest. His meal was not finished when a telephone message from Gorleston said the Yarmouth boat had been damaged and in the event of another call the Cromer boat might be wanted. So Henry Blogg, the mechanic and E. Hansell (the secretary) hurried back to Yarmouth.

They arrived there at 3 p.m. and found that the *H. F. Bailey* was not at the quayside. Events had indeed moved very fast since they left that morning! The Great Yarmouth and Gorleston boat *John and Mary Meiklam* had answered a distress-call from the *Yewbank*, of Glasgow, which had run ashore near Horsey Point. This was obviously the ship the Cromer men had seen as they came in from the service to the *Nesttun*.

A dangerous heavy sea was breaking all around the *Yewbank*. The Yarmouth boat approached cautiously to judge the best method of rescue. They had drawn close to the ship when a hissing, curling breaker swept at them and, taking them by surprise, broke aboard the lifeboat. It was as though a mountain of green water toppled on to them. It flattened every man and washed two of the crew overboard. The boat rolled, as though to shake off the burden of water. The decks ran like a sluice and all the relieving scuppers spouted.

One of the men swept into the water had for some reason just taken off his lifebelt. The second man, however, reached him and tried to support him in the water.

As if that was not trouble enough for the crew, the steering-wheel gear was damaged and it was with much difficulty that the coxswain manoeuvred the boat. He picked up his men, however, but it took fifteen minutes to do so.

The efficiency of the kapok lifebelt was proved here for two men, heavy with water, oilskins and sea-boots, were kept afloat with one belt for that length of time.

One man was blue in the face and unconscious when hauled aboard. Artificial respiration was immediately applied and maintained until he revived. While this was happening another fierce wave lunged at the *John and Mary Meiklam* and completely wrecked the steering gear. The lifeboat was getting near the breaking surf and was uncontrollable. Disaster seemed almost certain, but the mechanic saved the situation by scrambling up and along the stern-box of the boat and while his legs were held by other members of the crew he worked feverishly until the wheel-gear had been freed from the rudder. This allowed hand steering to be used and as he clambered back the coxswain was yelling orders and the boat was again under control.

Destruction had been averted but there was nothing they could do now for the *Yewbank*. They turned reluctantly and struggled home, arriving about midday. The men who had been overboard were given medical attention.

Meanwhile, life-saving apparatus was set up on shore and the crew of the *Yewbank*, who had been dismayed at the mishap to the lifeboat, were saved.

To add to this excitement Cromer No. 2 boat *Harriot Dixon* was called out to a barge, the *Lady Gwynfred*, of London, which had also run aground north of Cromer. While the lifeboat was being launched a rearing 'seventh' caught her, washed her off the carriage and swept her ashore. Her dazed crew were just sorting themselves out after this mishap when news was received that the *Lady Gwynfred*'s crew had also been rescued from the shore. That was the abrupt end of the third launching.

At 1 p.m. a drifter struggled into Gorleston harbour with the tragic news that she had seen in the distance a huge wave catch another drifter broadside. It had turned turtle.

The position given was half a mile north-west of Corton light-vessel.

The *John and Mary Meiklam* could not be used safely owing to her damaged steering, but the *H. F. Bailey* lay in the harbour, so the Yarmouth crew manned the Cromer boat. The man who had been washed overboard that morning and had supported his comrade in the water was among the crew.

The gale was then at its full fury, but the lifeboat diligently searched the spot, although taking green seas herself. They found no trace of the capsized drifter, later identified as the *Olive Branch*, of Peterhead. Although her crew of nine had practically no chance of surviving in such a storm, strange things can and do happen at sea, so the lifeboat continued to beat around until all doubt was removed.

That was the news the Cromer men heard when they got back to Yarmouth at 3 p.m. and found their boat gone. They waited on the quayside until she came in at 5 p.m. with the grim report that the *Olive Branch* was lost with all hands.

The fifth call came at 7 p.m. Another drifter was in trouble. The storm had already crippled her and a sister boat was towing her to the harbour when the tow broke and the seas began pushing her towards the shore. The Gorleston secretary gave authority to call his crew and in five minutes the *H. F. Bailey* with the Yarmouth crew, Henry Blogg and his mechanic on board, was putting away from the quayside.

They soon found the boat struggling to avoid capsizing as she drifted engine-less towards the beach, a mile from Gorleston pier. It was the Banff steam-drifter *Pitagavenny* with ten men on board. As soon as her tow parted she heaved anchor, but it would not hold.

To get alongside the pitching and rolling *Pitagavenny* was a risky manoeuvre. Her rudder swung from side to side, locking first one way then the other, while the boat zigzagged accordingly. The Yarmouth coxswain had two runs at it and failed. Henry Blogg took the wheel and tried twice without success. He then judged his opportunity, yelled to the crew 'Stand ready,' and ran the lifeboat straight at the drifter as though to ram her. Then, when almost up to the target, he swung the lifeboat hard to starboard, bringing the side of the *H. F. Bailey* against the *Pitagavenny* with a bump that stove in a bow-plank. Ropes made the lifeboat fast in a flash and the rescue began.

The Scotch drifter had rough balks of wood for fenders and these gave the lifeboat many a body-punch as she was held alongside, but the ten men were taken off and the lifeboat turned for Yarmouth.

The Cromer boat was back in harbour looking a bit battered but game for further calls by 8.15 p.m. The lifeboatmen, however, after that hectic day, were glad of a quiet spell. This lasted until the small hours of November 19 and then the call was very different – the SS *Yewforest* of Glasgow, lying in the Roads, was flying a signal asking for a doctor.

The gale had eased but the sea was still churlish and ill-tempered. A doctor offered his services and the Gorleston secretary was again consulted. The *H. F. Bailey*, manned as before, went out at 8.20 a.m. and put the doctor on board.

As they led him below to a cabin they told him what had happened. It was an unusual accident. At the height of the gale a fireman had been pitched down the fo'c'sle steps. The doctor looked at the injured man but did not open his case. There was nothing he could do. The man was dead.

They brought the doctor back and when the lifeboat moored at the quay the clock showed 9.35. The crew were just climbing ashore when the coastguard dashed to them with the message that a ship passing through the Cockle Gat was on fire and help was urgently needed. Within five minutes of coming alongside the quay the *H. F. Bailey* was on her way again for the seventh launch. The crew arrangements were unaltered.

They found the Newcastle steamer *Lindisfarne* tossing at anchor in Yarmouth Roads. She was on fire and her crew were trying desperately to prevent the flames reaching the highly inflammable cargo of matches, chocolates and toys.

Henry Blogg went on board and Captain J. Hervey, who was

very anxious because the fire would soon be beyond control, asked the lifeboat to bring help from HMS *Foyle* which was lying near by. Henry Blogg remained on the *Lindisfarne* while the *H. F. Bailey* went to the naval vessel and returned through the rough sea with a fire party.

The lifeboat then stood by until the fire had been extinguished. The fire-party was safely collected and taken back to Yarmouth to rejoin HMS *Foyle*. As soon as he was ashore Henry Blogg telephoned for two members of his crew to come from Cromer to help in getting the lifeboat home.

On November 20 the *H. F. Bailey* left the sprawling, still sleeping port of Gorleston at 4.45 a.m. and arrived at her own slipway four hours later. She had been on five missions in four days of gales. Now, she found it good to settle down in her own boathouse, rub her many bruises and reflect on the hectic existence of a lifeboat. From 11.12 a.m. on November 16 until 3.40 p.m. on

The H. F. Bailey *lifeboat (1935-45) with Henry Blogg at the helm, preparing to rehouse on the pier. This lifeboat is now on display at the Henry Blogg Lifeboat Museum at Cromer.*

November 19, seventy-six hours, Cromer's two boats had been at sea for sixty-two hours. Sixty-year-old Henry Blogg had been out for fifty-two hours in almost continuous rough weather, wet through most of the time and shouldering a very heavy responsibility.

11

The *Cantabria*

THE SERVICE to the Spanish steamer *Cantabria* on November 2, 1938, was not an epic rescue for the Cromer lifeboat, for the weather was fine, the sea calm and there were no great hazards to face. The tragic story is told because it shows that, even on the most unlikely day, when the Cromer crew were wanted they were ready and carried out a delicate task with efficiency. It also shows Henry Blogg's dislike of exaggerated reports.

At Cromer it is when the north-east gale is blowing and the breakers, with the weight of the North Sea behind them, are pounding the beach that the lifeboat-men expect a call. But out of a serene sky can come sudden drama and urgency. Then, whatever the task, the coxswain and each member of the crew must get to the boat-house without tying the loose ends of the job he is on. It was the crashing of maroons and the puffs of white smoke against the November sky that sent the crew dashing to the pier and told Cromer that her boat was needed.

The service to the *Cantabria* was the grim forerunner of what was shortly to follow – war. This call was not to save men from the wrath of the sea, but from the hatred of their fellow men and women and children were mixed up in the grim affair. Not since 1904, when Russian ships fired on British fishermen thinking they were Japanese torpedo boats, had foreign guns been heard in the North Sea during peace.

Barely two months had passed since Europe had stood on the brink of another world war. The Munich crisis was still painfully fresh in memory and if the haunting word 'war' was not on every one's tongue it was at the back of every one's mind. Mr Chamberlain had come back with his slip of paper and triumphant assurance 'Peace in our time,' but people were still very uneasy and when the dull crash of gunfire was heard that afternoon a score of questions sprang to every tongue.

But this was not Hitler's war – although he had a bony finger in it. It was a brutal reminder on our own doorstep of what was happening on the Iberian Peninsula. It was murder on the high seas – the attack on an unarmed vessel by an armed auxiliary cruiser.

The SS *Cantabria* was a ship of 5649 tons, registered at Santander and built in 1919. She was one of several Spanish vessels which were arrested and became the centre of a High Court battle for ownership. The Spanish Government had won the case and the ship had been chartered to the Mid-Atlantic Shipping Company, of London. She had unloaded a cargo of Russian timber in the Thames and had left on Tuesday morning in ballast and was proceeding to Immingham, bound for Leningrad.

There were on board forty-five crew and passengers, including three women and five children – one only three years old. Captain Aguelles had with him his wife Trinidad, his son Ramon, aged six and little Veyona, a girl of eight.

The *Cantabria* was proceeding north, following the coastline about four miles out, when at 11.30 a.m. Captain Aguelles noticed that a distant ship appeared to be following him. He altered course several degrees to see if there was any corresponding change in the other vessel and after a few minutes he noted with uneasiness that a similar change occurred. His officers scanned the stranger and agreed with their captain that it appeared to be an ordinary passenger vessel of about 1500 tons.

But they were wrong. The shadowing ship was in fact the *Nadir*, an auxiliary cruiser of General Franco's fleet. Five guns, concealed by false boarding, gave the Nadir a harmless appearance that enabled her to get close to her prey without revealing her intentions.

The binoculars of the officers of the *Cantabria* did not penetrate the disguise of the trailing vessel, but everything about her behaviour was disquieting. Captain Aguelles turned towards the Norfolk coast, hoping the other vessel would continue its previous course and get farther from the shore. But the *Nadir* also turned and increased her speed. The anxious captain saw a flag running up to the masthead of the following ship and recognised it as the flag of the Spanish Insurgents. His fears were confirmed. Then he read the signal in international code: 'Heave to or I fire.' Even as he read the signal he saw the activity on the ship's decks as the mask was removed and the naked guns of the *Nadir* revealed.

The next phase of the drama brought in a lot of spectators, startled ones at that, for the *Nadir* followed up its threat by a couple of rounds of gunfire. The sound waves rolled landward and windows rattled and houses shook all along the nearby coast. Both shells fell wide of the mark, but the will to kill was there.

It was now nearly 3 p.m. In Cromer, Sheringham and the little fishing-villages along the coast people stopped in the streets or came out of their houses; fishermen rose from mending nets and crab-pots, faces appeared at hotel windows looking towards the sea and from the shops folk hurried into the streets asking, 'What's happening?' 'What was that?'

Workers sugar-beeting in the fields also hurried to vantage points overlooking the sea. Coastguards and other watchers with binoculars clearly saw the two vessels, then a mile apart and about ten miles north of Cromer. The gun-flashes could be seen by the naked eye.

These were not the only watchers, for the *Nadir*'s guns had startled the fishing-fleet, which was proceeding to the fishing-grounds, taking but little interest in the two bigger ships. The crack of guns, however, brought everyone rushing to the rails to see what was going on. When other shells sent up columns of water near the *Cantabria* the fishermen realised that mischief was afoot and decided to show their disapproval. They did not know the cause of the quarrel, but as one ship flew the Spanish flag and the other the Insurgents' it was obviously no tea party. As one man the fishing-trawlers turned off their course towards the attacking ship and, with sirens hurling noisy if not specific abuse, censured this example of modern savagery.

The *Nadir* knew the fishing-vessels could not harm her, but the group of little ships belching angry smoke and screaming denunciation made a disquieting sight. She shifted course and made off, as though quitting the scene. Such was not her intention, however, and as soon as the trawlers had swung back to their original course, with many a salty epithet hurled at the retreating raider, the *Nadir* returned to her prey.

As soon as she was back within range she let fly at the *Cantabria* and the windows shook again along the coast. This time her shooting was more accurate, an one of the shells struck the bridge. In a welter of splintering glass and wood Captain Aguelles and his mate flung themselves to the deck. Apart from small cuts and bruises, neither was hurt, but much of the bridge was wrecked. The wheel was smashed and communication with the engine-room was gone. The vessel heeled and shuddered as the shell struck and the alarm of the passengers was pitiable. The dark-haired Spanish women who had been told to stay in their cabins clutched their children as though to put their bodies between the infants and the flying splinters. The alarmed crew rushed from one shelter to another, trying to keep as much of the ship as possible between them and the guns as the *Nadir* circled the steamer.

The renewed outburst of gunfire set the folk on land guessing again and those with binoculars saw that the larger ship had been struck. They did not know what the dispute was about but they knew with tingling apprehension that it was an act of war. There was, however, more than alarm; there was an outburst of indignation, for although Englishmen have their share of faults they do not do things this way. The sight of one ship shelling another obviously unarmed vessel went against every feeling of decency. The onlookers could not give vent to their feelings as loudly as the fishing-boats had done but they were no less emphatic.

The *Nadir* continued circling and firing. She scored a decisive hit when a shell penetrated the engine-room and stopped the engines. The *Cantabria* was now helpless. One of the crew was seriously hurt, not by the actual explosion but through falling into the gaping stokehold. He was rescued and given what aid was possible. The rebel ship followed up her successes by raking her victim with machine-gun fire, but – apart from causing greater terror among the passengers – this did little harm. Whether the captain of the insurgent ship knew there were women and children on board is not certain. Whether it would have made any difference is problematic. We in this country had been shocked and horrified by the cruelty and bitterness of the Spanish Civil War; the massacre of priests and the fearful bombing of Guernica were incomprehensible to us and out here in the North Sea, off our own coast, we heard the echo of that pitiless struggle.

The women and children on the stricken ship expected any moment that a shell would blow them to pieces. They saw death in every gun-flash. The crew too had had more than enough and begged the captain to surrender the vessel. This he refused to do, but continued to dodge from side to side of the ship so that, like the crew, he could put the greatest thickness of iron between himself and the attacker.

The radio-operator of the *Cantabria* continued sending messages. His message 'Being shelled by unknown vessel' was the first warning that something nasty was afoot. This message was received by the SS *Monkwood* and broadcast. A wireless fan in Lowestoft picked it up and the Humber radio station soon confirmed it. Another message stated that a cruiser was flying the signal 'Heave to or I fire.'

Then, when the bridge and engines were smashed, the radio operator sent out an SOS giving his position as eight and a half miles south-west of Haisbro' light-vessel. The *Cantabria* was

Cromer lifeboat crew, with Henry Blogg shaking the hand of Captain Aguelles of the Cantabria.

holed in many places and water poured into her. The daylight was beginning to fade and soon darkness would add to their plight.

A message to Cromer asked for lifeboat aid. So, to add to the drama, there came the boom of the maroons over Cromer and the hurrying of the crew along the resounding planks of the pier. Henry Blogg was just recovering from an attack of appendicitis and could not hurry.

It was five o'clock and nearly dark when the *H. F. Bailey* slid down the slipway and sliced into a smooth sea to make a perfect launch. Henry Blogg gave his orders crisply, for although there was little wind to hinder and only moderate seas, there was no time to lose. If the wireless messages were not exaggerated another lucky shell from the attacker could sink the *Cantabria* with all on board.

In point of fact, the position of the steamer had so far worsened that a fire had started below decks and the crew had decided to quit their ship. Two boats were lowered and the women and children who wanted to go were first put into them, most of them weeping and trembling with fright. For hours they had been subjected to shelling and machine-gunning and to this terror were added the fears of fire on board and night approaching. One boat was prepared to surrender to the attacker and moved towards it, but the other preferred the open sea to the mercies of the Insurgents and pulled away from both the *Cantabria* and the *Nadir*.

Captain Aguelles had no intention of putting himself into the hands of the *Nadir*. The men who would sink a helpless ship with women and children on board were not likely to respect any conventions about prisoners. He preferred to stay on his ship and take the consequences. The captain's wife, his two children and the second steward, Joaquin Vallego, refused to leave him. As the two boats pulled away those five looked down with strange feelings, wondering what would become of them.

The *Nadir*, seeing the boats being lowered, stopped firing. It was nearly 4.15 and outlined on the horizon another ship was drawing nearer; the steamer *Pattersonian*, bound for London, had heard the SOS appeals of the *Cantabria* and now approached the battered steamer. The *Nadir* attempted to intervene and a collision was only just averted. As one boat was pulling towards the *Pattersonian* her engines were stopped and as the boat came alongside ropes and rope-ladders were thrown and one by one the eleven Spaniards came on board.

The captain of the *Pattersonian* waited until he saw the Cromer lifeboat heading for the stationary ship, then – with his quota of rescued – continued his journey and put the Spaniards into Yarmouth.

As the lifeboat hastened through the increasing darkness to the scene of the drama no more shots were fired. The *Cantabria* was showing no lights but sending up a column of smoke and steam. When Henry Blogg arrived at about 6.30 he realised that if he was going to take off anyone on that ship there must be no delay. Captain Aguelles discerned the lifeboat approaching and gave light-signals with a torch. The *Cantabria* then had an ugly starboard list. The lifeboat drew alongside and the captain hailed him in English. A line was thrown which the steward caught. Señora Trinidad Aguelles, followed by fair-haired six-year-old Ramon and Veyona in a bright woollen coat and with yellow ribbons in her dark hair, was handed down into the lifeboat, then the steward and finally the captain. As the Spaniards were being rescued the ship heeled over and bore down upon the lifeboat, damaging her stanchions, so that the *H. F. Bailey* hastened to get away. The lifeboat went towards the *Nadir*, but the crew shouted in English, 'Get away. We are Spanish. We do not want you.'

The steamer heeled right over and her starboard deck went under the water; holed and scarred, she was heeling at an angle of fifty degrees and clouds of steam and smoke swirled about her. The lifeboat got well away and as Henry Blogg looked back he saw the ship begin to settle into the sea. Then, in a smother of spray and steam, she sank, flinging up spouts of water and pieces of wreckage. The sea churned and swirled as the mass of iron and wood went down and released air forced its way to the surface.

The *Nadir* made no attempt to interfere. Her work was done. She had used up an immense amount of ammunition and her deed was nothing to boast about, even to other captains of the Franco fleet. The Spanish Government, however, had lost a useful ship and orders had been obeyed. It was time to sheer off.

The *H. F. Bailey* made good time homeward through the darkness, reaching her slipway at 8.15 p.m. The relief of Señora Aguelles at finding herself on land with her children and husband safe can only be imagined. She was a brave woman whom the War had already hit hard, for she had fled from three different homes and now had lost all but the clothes she stood in. The hours of acute danger had left their mark. Her face was drawn, her hair dishevelled. But soon the friendliness of all around and the prospect of food and drink brought reassurance. Her thanks were profuse. To

Henry Blogg she poured out a torrent of words which undoubtedly conveyed her gratitude but otherwise meant nothing to him. He pulled his cloth cap over his eyes and began to remove his lifebelt while the survivors were being taken to an hotel.

The captain was anxious about the safety of his crew, but over the radio came the answer that the *Pattersonian* had anchored in Yarmouth Roads and the Gorleston lifeboat had taken on board eleven members of the *Cantabria*'s crew. The account of the incident was followed by a BBC warning to shipping, giving the sunken ship's location.

As soon as the rescued Spaniards had rested and relaxed a reporter was admitted with an interpreter. Through the interpreter Captain Aguelles told his story. He had, however, only answered one or two questions when his little daughter Veyona, who had bottled up far too long her side of the affair, could contain herself no longer and suddenly interposed, 'I was the oldest of the children. So I just couldn't be afraid. The others all wanted to go to the other ship, but I didn't want to go. I wanted to stay with Daddy and Mummy. I didn't see the fire, but I don't think I want to go to sea again.'

The eleven men landed at Yarmouth were taken to the sailors' home. Newspaper reporters arrived quickly to get their version of the shooting, but although one member of the crew who could speak a little English was ready to talk not one of the rescued men would be photographed, for they feared Franco would see the photograph and take some revenge. The men had good reason to fear the Insurgents, for they had barely escaped with their lives and had lost everything except the clothes they stood in. Crowds waited at Yarmouth and Cromer to catch a glimpse of the Spaniards. The national newspapers carried banner-headlines and while the country read the story in graphic detail and questions were asked in Parliament, Henry Blogg and his crew went back to braiding their crab-pot nets. One report stated that the lifeboat went to the rescue through a hail of gunfire and that 'Shells were plopping in the sea about her,' but Henry Blogg was not accepting credit for such fictitious gallantry. 'We didn't hear a gun fired on the journey out or back,' he corrected. The Cromer lifeboat had done another job of work efficiently and but for their prompt action that ugly incident would have been stained with the deaths of brave Señora Aguelles and little Veyona, who 'would not have gone to sea again'.

12

The *Mount Ida*

ONLY A MONTH had passed since Mr Neville Chamberlain had announced to a stunned nation that Britain was at war with Germany when the Cromer crew hit the headlines with another magnificent rescue. This time, as though tired of so many trips to the Haisborough Sands, they went thirty miles out into the North Sea on their mercy mission to the *Mount Ida*.

In many ways this rescue was Henry Blogg's greatest achievement in seamanship – and that is saying a lot. Had it not been for his amazing skill in handling the lifeboat, some or the things he did on this service could have been called foolhardy. But, more than any other man, he knew just what could be done with a modern lifeboat and he was as much at home in a North Sea gale as a London bus driver in the rush-hour traffic. Half a dozen things about this rescue should have beaten him – had he ever known when he was beaten.

October 9, 1939, was wet and windy with a dreary mist over the sea. At 6.30 a.m. Humber radio station informed Cromer coastguard that another ship had run aground on the Haisborough Sands. That was a routine job for the crew – or so it seemed – then. They had almost made a track across the trackless waters to those sands.

Henry Blogg was already astir and was lighting the fire in Swallow Cottage when the telephone rang. He dropped his sticks by the blue-tiled fireplace to take the call.

The crew could not be called by maroons as they had been banned during the War, so Ann went off in the rain to warn the near-by members of the crew while Henry Blogg called the others and then ran on to the boat-house.

But the coastguard had beaten him and was already opening the big doors. The tide was at half ebb and an unusually heavy sea was running. The wind was south-east by east and getting stronger. Conditions were anything but pleasant but they had all seen worse.

Despite the difficulty of calling the crew the *H. F. Bailey* hit the water within twenty minutes of the decision to launch. Of the twelve men in the lifeboat when she plunged down her slip-way nine were Davies, two were named Cox and the skipper, of course, was Henry Blogg.

Before they slid out into the sea Henry Blogg asked the coast-guard to try and get more details about the location of the vessel and to inform him or the light-vessel by radio.

The *H. F. Bailey* throbbed her way south-eastward through a difficult sea, rising and falling like a sea-bird, but thrusting her shining white bows through the hissing green water all the time towards the North Middle Haisborough Sands.

An hour after launching and when the boat had battled ten or eleven miles under the wind-blown sky, the mechanic who was listening attentively to the radio heard the words 'Ower. Ower.' It was the Cromer coastguard talking to the light-vessel, but they had clawed part of the message out of the spray and rain-filled air and it was clear that the instructions were that the wreck was not on the Haisborough Sands but on the Ower Bank nine-teen miles farther out, with the dangerous Leman Bank lying between. *How prophetic*

The restrictions on radio conversation during wartime for-bade further talk, so, without wasting precious time by going to the light-vessel, Henry Blogg swung south to pick up the Middle Haisbro' buoy. From there he was able to turn eastward across the sands to a gap between that one and the East Haisbro' buoy. He then turned the bows on a north-east course for the Ower Bank, still some thirteen miles away and threaded his way among the sands like a taxi-driver through the streets of Soho.

Their wives and children back in Cromer were sitting down to dinner when the crew were taking the lifeboat through a narrow channel between the treacherous shallows of the Leman Bank, four miles short of the Ower. The seas were growing worse, with the wind whipping the crest of the breakers into spray.

They had come through several sharp rain-squalls, but now it was clear and in the distance they saw across the waste of heaving water a large vessel on the middle of the Bank, almost in the position that Henry Blogg had told the crew he had expected to find it.

As they drew nearer they read *Mount Ida* on the bows. It was a 4275-ton Greek vessel of Piraeus. She had crossed the Atlantic from Vancouver with a mixed cargo, mostly timber and grain, due for unloading at Hull. She carried a crew of twenty-nine.

In the hours taken by the lifeboat to reach the stranded ship the North Sea had already left its mark. Savage waves were breaking on the Bank and leaping so high at the throat of the ship that they had already plucked off two lifeboats and ripped through most of the bridge. The cargo had shifted and the Mount Ida had an ugly starboard list. Things looked very unpleasant and the task of rescue at first sight seemed impossible.

Henry Blogg sized up the situation and realised this was to be a stern test of his seamanship. The wreck was lying head-on to the breakers, so there was no lee for the lifeboat. The great waves were hitting the bows and running along both sides of the ship. He hoped, however, he could get a line aboard on the port side and with great care approached the ship. The bowman was just swaying back to heave his hand-line when two breakers in quick succession hurled the *H. F. Bailey* back, nearly flinging the bowman into the sea.

Both Henry Blogg and Jack Davies were at the wheel trying to hold the boat steady. Together they brought the lifeboat round in another attempt. It failed. The big ship had set up such powerful cross-currents with the tide that the lifeboat could not stay alongside. The seas came rolling in from all directions.

One unwary moment and the *H. F. Bailey* could be caught against the side of the *Mount Ida* and smashed to matchwood. Henry Blogg therefore decided he must wait for the tide to drop.

For all his daring, Henry Blogg did not invite destruction. He could see that the position of the *Mount Ida*, although bad, was not yet desperate. He was content to bide his time. So he told Henry Davies to signal his intention to stand off and moved away from the troubled Bank into deeper and appreciably quieter water. There he stayed and dodged – not anchored, but with engines just maintaining a headway against the seas.

For nearly two hours the lifeboat-men rode out the heavy seas, watching with unslacking vigilance the masses of water that moved relentlessly against them. Sometimes, for all they could do, the seas broke right over the boat and every man had to cling for life to whatever was nearest. The gulls wheeled and screamed above them, as though they too were alarmed at this duel with death.

Without mishap, however, the time passed until Henry Blogg felt justified in making a further attempt. The tide had dropped, although the wind and seas seemed even rougher. But the afternoon was wearing fast away and the darkness would be no friend. It was time to move in.

Round came the wheel and the blue-and-white bows with the coxswain, tensely anxious, gripping the spokes and shouting quick instructions to his crew. Watchful for the menace of each approaching wave, and with consummate skill and judgement, Henry Blogg put the lifeboat alongside the Greek ship.

On the *Mount Ida* the captain and crew watched anxiously the manoeuvres of the lifeboat, realising that their lives hung upon the seamanship and courage of these foreigners in oilskins below them.

As soon as the *H. F. Bailey* was alongside, the Greek seamen flung down the ropes from the ship and rapidly they were made fast. For a moment it looked as if they had solved the problem, that the rescue could go ahead, but when a rushing sea tore the boat from the side of the wreck the terrific strain broke both ropes. Quickly, one after another, more ropes were thrown and secured, but each time the pull of the snarling seas snapped the thick ropes like thread. When more than twelve ropes had been fastened and parted it was obvious the boat could not be held alongside by that method and it looked as though the seas had beaten them. But Henry Blogg had not yet played all his cards. If he could not use ropes then he would try using the two powerful engines of his boat to hold the *H. F. Bailey* in position.

It was a bold plan and the risk was tremendous. If it failed he might smash his boat, lose the lives of his crew and leave the twenty-nine desperate men without hope of rescue. On the other hand, he could not leave the *Mount Ida*'s men while even the smallest chance of survival remained. He believed the risk justified and every man of his crew was prepared to trust their coxswain's judgement.

As the waves broke in foaming cascades against the towering steel sides of the ship, Henry Blogg drove 'full ahead' with both engines and prevented the seas from carrying him away, or 'slow ahead' with port and 'full ahead' with starboard engine to help him keep the bows from swinging against the riveted flank of the *Mount Ida*.

The Greeks also acted quickly and dropped a rope ladder hastily over the rail. Five men clambered down as far as they could, then jumped on to the lifeboat deck. The sixth man mistimed his jump and fell between the *H. F. Bailey* and the steamer. In a flash Robert Cox had flung the man a rope and lifebuoy. With panic in his eyes the man struggled to reach it. It swept past him, he tried again and grasped the bobbing circle of salvation. Two men drew him in and hauled him over the bulging cork fender into the lifeboat, a great coughing, retching human 'fish'.

All this did not help the next man. He had clambered over the steamer's rails and had seen what happened. He got halfway down the swaying ladder when his nerve broke; he hesitated and then shakily began to climb back to the wreck. The crew of the lifeboat yelled like madmen above the roar of the sea for him to jump, but even if he understood that strange northern tongue it made no difference. He had almost got to the rail when a mountain of seething green-and-white water lifted the *H. F. Bailey* as high as the top of the ladder and banged it against him as he climbed desperately to get away from the roaring sea. He was caught between a twenty-ton hammer and a 4000-ton anvil, between mahogany and steel and his legs were dreadfully mangled. His comrades grabbed him, even as he screamed and flung up his arms. They dragged him, sobbing and writhing, on board the *Mount Ida*.

This was a tragic and unwanted complication, but just the sort of incalculable element that arises in the lifeboat service and makes a text-book useless. It was a horrible and unusual accident that no one could have prevented.

What should be done now? The man was in terrible agony, but there were twenty-two other lives in jeopardy. The only thing that seemed most right was to treat the injured man and risk the delay. The Greeks tried to staunch the flow of blood with tourniquets. Then they rolled the man in blankets for warmth and, taking him to the steamer's port lifeboat, prepared to lower him by ropes. It was rough treatment for a mangled body but there was no alternative.

Henry Blogg moved a little farther from the dangerous proximity of the ship until he saw what the Greeks were doing. Then he brought the *H. F. Bailey* alongside beneath the ship's boat and maintained her there as nearly as he could by his engines.

The moaning bundle of humanity was lowered as gently as possible in those grim conditions and laid in the aft cockpit. The lifeboat-men had seen much of the sea's cruelty but it had not made them hard. Their rough hands were surprisingly tender as they gave the sufferer a swig of rum and one of the lifeboat crew took off his own much-needed coat and folded it to pillow the stranger's head. Then, as this seemed the safest method, the rest of the Greek crew slid down the rope after clambering from the ship into their boat hanging from its davits.

Even in those grim moments there was a flare of humour when one of the Greeks slid off the rope and sat on the top of the lifeboat exhaust-funnel.

It was nearly four o'clock when Henry Blogg turned to leave the stout Greek ship and her valuable cargo to the waves. He could not save that much-needed grain and wood or the more-needed ship, but he had saved twenty-nine seamen and it had been worth the risk.

The injured man could not be got into shelter out of the biting wind, but his Greek shipmates squatted around him in a circle, taking the wind themselves to break it for him. Holding on to anything handy in the tossing lifeboat, they made a human wall. They remained like that for over two hours. In that lifeboat-man's coat and their silent sacrifice we see examples of the true brother-hood of the sea.

Henry Blogg had held his boat against the *Mount Ida* for an hour, using her engines to maintain his station and, for all his skill, nothing could prevent the seas knocking her into the flank of the ship. The lifeboat was inevitably badly damaged by such buffeting, although the deep cork fender had suffered many blows.

Such a daring, determined, brilliant manoeuvre summed up the seamanship of Henry Blogg. It was also a tribute to the skill with which the mechanics had nursed their engines and carried out the coxswain's orders as quickly he gave them.

But the job was not over, for they had yet to get themselves off the Ower Bank. Not only was the lifeboat damaged but the tide had run very low on the sands. The lifeboat also was loaded with the additional weight of twenty-nine men and it would mean dis-aster if she grounded in these shallow waters. They were so far out to sea that the sandbanks were strange to Henry Blogg. He decided that boldness must be his ally. 'Full ahead,' he called to his mechanics and the lifeboat immediately responded with the propellers giving their maximum thrust and lift.

With a tense feeling at his throat Henry Blogg sped straight ahead at the seas. If they grounded at speed it would be fatal, if

Before the acquisition of a motor tractor, the Harriot Dixon *had to be launched by hand until the boat was in deep enough water to be floated off her wheeled carriage. Henry Blogg is supervising the launch.*

they went gingerly they would be heavier in the water. Daring paid. Although they may well have scraped the paint off the bottom of the keel, they cleared the Ower Bank. Then came the next problem. For what port should they steer?

It was unlikely that they could berth at Cromer in the seas that were still running, but it was the nearest point and Henry Blogg felt he ought to land the badly injured man as soon as possible. The Greek had lost a great deal of blood and, apart from that, the shock and exposure were enough to kill him. Yet they were thirty miles away from Cromer and, though he put on the best speed, it was 8 p.m. when they arrived off the slipway.

As Henry Blogg had feared, there was no chance of getting even near enough to the slipway to land the injured man. The only way to get over this new difficulty was to launch the *Harriot Dixon* from the beach, for she could get back even in that sea. Accordingly the No. 2 boat was pulled to the water's edge by her tractor and launched in the dark about 8.30 p.m. and on board her was the doctor who was to attend Henry Blogg in his last illness.

During this launching another unfortunate accident occurred. If there are 'gremlins' for lifeboats they were very active on this service, for one thing after another seemed to go wrong. This time a throttle wire broke and the engine stalled. Only a little thing, but it happened at a crucial moment, just when the boat was being launched. Left momentarily helpless, an incoming breaker picked her up like a cork and threw her broadside almost on her beam-ends across the carriage, knocking a hole in her side and breaking the carriage. The crew and doctor were thrown all over the place but they quickly rallied and, with many helpers in the water, launched the boat again, stern first. Although damaged, she got to the *H. F. Bailey* and took off the injured man with the rest of *Mount Ida*'s crew and the crew of No. 1 boat. Four of the *Harriot Dixon*'s crew stayed on the *H. F. Bailey* with her own mechanic to watch while she rode out the storm.

The injured Greek was rushed to Cromer Hospital where they did all they could for him, but his injuries were so severe he died the next night. That moment of hesitation on the ladder had cost him his life.

The *H. F. Bailey*'s crew, which had been out fourteen hours, went home to a hot meal and dry clothes, but Henry Blogg stayed behind to direct the salving of the *Harriot Dixon*'s tractor and carriage, which were both completely submerged. It was dark and seas were breaking on them, but a wire hawser was fixed and they were winched up the beach. Only when this had at last been done did Henry Blogg go home. With slow, tired step he climbed the cliff, turned into Corner Street and let himself into Swallow Cottage. Ann was just helping him off with his wet clothes and boots when the door-bell rang. A young fisherman stood there breathless. Another vessel was in trouble down the coast at Bacton, ten miles away. Henry Blogg told the man to call the crew out again and quickly got into some dry clothes himself. Without taking his meal, he hurried to the boathouse to see to the refuelling of the *H. F. Bailey* from the slipway at the end of the pier. It was soon obvious, however, that the darkness and high seas made this impossible. They could not use the *Harriot Dixon* because of the accident, so the largest crab-boat was launched and loaded with forty tins of petrol. Then the *H. F. Bailey's* crew went out to their boat. When the crew and the fuel had been transferred, two of the lifeboat-men brought the crab-boat back. The 'gremlins' were still busy, for as they were returning with the heavy boat the surf caught them and the hearts of the watchers almost stopped as the boat heeled over in an instant and it looked as if she must capsize. She hovered, undecided and then righted herself.

Meanwhile, H. W. Davies was filling his almost exhausted petrol-tanks from the fresh supply and the *H. F. Bailey* started down the coast to Bacton. The sea had moderated a little, but it was raining and a strong wind was still blowing from the southeast.

It was the *Vera Creina* of Lowestoft, a steam-drifter, that was in distress. She had been making for her home port from the fishing-grounds with her crew of ten when she got into difficulty and ran aground.

It was 1 a.m. on October 10 when the *H. F. Bailey* arrived and the crew could see moving lights on the shore and hear voices hailing them. Henry Blogg strained his ears to catch the message above the noise of wind and surf. It was good news; the crew of ten had been rescued by rocket apparatus.

As he was now well on his way to Lowestoft where the damaged boat would have to be repaired, Henry Blogg decided to carry on rather than return to Cromer and then have to take the boat to Lowestoft later. The sooner she was repaired the better in case of further need.

But Lowestoft was twenty-five miles down the coast and they were all feeling very exhausted. However, that was the sensible course, so the *H. F. Bailey* carried on to Lowestoft and reached there at 6.30 a.m. Her stem was badly damaged and ribs, deck-beams and sides had been broken. Twenty feet of fender had been torn off, the gunwale split all along the starboard side and stanchions bent and broken. It was twenty-four hours earlier that they had set out to help the *Mount Ida*, they had been afloat for twenty-one hours and had travelled more than a hundred miles.

Henry Blogg stands on Cromer pier with his second cox Jack Davies.

This long and hazardous service brought sixty-three-year-old Henry Blogg a third clasp to his Silver Medal to add to his two Gold Medals. In the Institution's 115 years no other man had such an achievement to his credit.

Second coxswain Jack Davies won a third service clasp to his Bronze Medal and mechanics H. W. and J. W. Davies second service clasps to their Bronze Medals. The rest of the crew received the thanks of the Institution inscribed on vellum.

13

Convoy No. 559

THE EARLY YEARS of the war were the most exacting for Henry Blogg, not only in the number of calls, but most navigation-lights were extinguished and the numerous attacks on light-vessels by enemy aircraft made it necessary to replace these invaluable ships with large buoys. The restrictions on radio-talk also made the lifeboat's task much harder. In the home Ann still tried to please her husband by cooking the things he liked: pies and puddings, shortcakes and sponges; but the strain of wartime shopping, anxiety for Henry, the incessant ringing of the telephone and always being 'on call' began to have an effect upon her. Moreover, however demanding her own home, she always managed to visit her widowed mother and invalid brother and do what she could to help them. But she never lost her sense of humour and often when they were both dead-tired and the current and wind of life seemed against them, Ann would make some dry comment that would set Henry chuckling.

Ann typified the sly wit of Norfolk. Norfolk does not put many comedians on to the stage, but in factory, farm and fishing-fleet one finds her humorous natives – and the males have no monopoly of this gift.

With expressionless face she would relate some interview or telephone conversation that would amuse Henry Blogg as much as the highly paid comedians of the radio whom he liked to hear.

And the rare occasions when she really let herself go with racy tales of girlhood adventures were a delight to the listener and a surprise to those who thought they knew her.

She was a foil for her husband's silence, often chattering away in top gear while he listened, smiled and occasionally nodded. The war did nothing to loosen his tongue, for apart from every hoarding shouting 'Careless Talk Costs Lives', he knew there were many things best kept under his sou'wester.

It was the secrecy that necessarily prevails in wartime that screened one of Henry Blogg's greatest rescues, one that for dash and seamanship is surely unequalled. It added another Gold Medal to his already imposing collection and eighty-eight precious lives to the station's score. Had this exploit occurred in peacetime the Press of the world would have acclaimed it as an epic of daring and skill, but as Britain was at war the less occasion the enemy had to gloat over the loss of so many good ships the better. In the magnitude of the disaster and the magnificence of the rescue work the service to Convoy FS 559 is unrivalled.

It was a Dutch seaman who said, 'To me, Henry Blogg is the symbol of daring enterprise,' and if the great coxswain had never gone on any other service this rescue would still have earned him that tribute.

It happened in August, which in theory is one of the best months of the year, but which in reality often falls far short. It certainly was not living up to its reputation on August 5, 1941. A north-north-west gale was blowing, it was raining, it was cold and visibility was poor.

Through a rough sea came a blacked-out convoy of merchant-ships guarded by two destroyers of the Rosyth escort force and a trawler escort. It threaded its way down the East Coast through the darkness, with oilskin-clad lookouts peering into the ink-bottle of the night for submarines, E-boats, mines, aircraft and other evidence of man's inhumanity to man. But the greatest danger came from an older enemy – the Norfolk shoals.

When day dawned a grey sea mist merged the grey sky into

a grey sea. Visibility was so poor that the convoy groped rather than sailed round the Norfolk coast.

The commodore and the ships' captains cursed the blanket of mist and the fact that they were drawing near the deadly Haisborough Sands. They had seen the Dudgeon light-vessel long ago, but where was the Haisbro' light? Could it be that the tide had swept them farther to port than they expected? They would all feel much happier when they were south of Yarmouth. If it was not for this cursed bank of fog they could soon be sure of their whereabouts. However, there was comfort in numbers. The merchantmen were reassured by the presence of the naval vessels and the destroyers were glad that these old merchant sea dogs knew this treacherous coast so well. But the sandbanks cared not a rap for the White Ensign or the Red Duster. They would as soon snare a cruiser as a crab boat and a gold-braided commodore was no more respected than a cabin boy.

On that drab, wet, apology for an August morning the unstable sands waited for the ships that were passing so close, passing too close. And then, somewhere between the East and South Middle Haisbro' buoys, six merchantmen were suddenly trapped and as soon as the sands gripped them the 'grinders' began their savage work.

On six ships the helmsman cried, 'The ship does not answer the helm.' On six ships there was a frantic signal to the engine-room, 'Full speed astern,' and on six ships the propellers threshed the cold, heaving waters in vain. Their stern waves came sweeping from behind and lifted each ship farther on to the sands. From their bunks came tumbling in alarm a hundred seamen and captains not on watch hurried to the bridge from their cabins. Stokers got hasty orders to raise steam-pressure while ship's officers held hasty consultation as the mist swayed around them. From the sands came the seething roar of breakers that had found iron walls to bite on.

The consternation on the naval vessels, still safe in deep water, was little less than on the merchant-ships. The shepherds had let the wolf reach the flock. Signals flashed from ship to ship and wireless-operators sent crisp, coded morse signals to Yarmouth base and the Humber radio station.

Whether one ship followed the other into the toil of the sands is not clear. The keenest eye could not see far through that clinging mist. Perhaps they all were borne simultaneously by the push of the gale and the strong currents that run with the tide on to the banks. But there they lay, all within a short space of each other; the *Oxshott* and the *Deerwood*, of London, *Gallois*, of Rouen, *Taara*, of Pärnu, Estonia, *Aberhill*, of Methil, Fife and the *Paddy Hendly* on her maiden voyage. What a mouthful of jibes that would have made for Lord Haw-Haw!

It was 8 a.m. when the lifeboat service was brought into the picture. For security reasons details were scant, as there was no need to invite enemy aircraft to come and finish what the sands had begun. Henry Blogg was told several ships had run aground on the southern end of the Middle Haisborough and the need was desperate. He was to be discreet. So the crew of No. 1 boat were not told of their mission until they were off the slipway and No. 2 crew, with Lewis Harrison in charge, were merely told to wait an hour for the tide to drop and then follow to the sands. The mist had cleared considerably.

The *H. F. Bailey* made full speed with the wind behind her. When Henry Blogg told the crew what he knew, they guessed something big was afoot. Henry Davies told his father Billy Davies, 'We're going to see something today we've never seen before.' And he was right. This was the biggest job the Cromer men ever had to tackle.

Long before they reached the sands they heard the drone of aircraft and wondered if the enemy had already got wind of the disaster, but it was an RAF patrol sent up to guard the helpless convoy. As the lifeboat approached through the heavy seas the crew saw a sight happily never likely to be seen again in a lifetime. There, lying close together, were six big ships on the sands with their backs broken or only their bridges showing and the seas breaking over them.

One of the destroyers had already begun rescue work with its

Henry Blogg in 1941. He referred to this as his favourite photograph.

whaler. It had been launched 'in steep breaking seas in which it was not expected any boat could live,' said the official report. That whaler had started its rescue operation at eight o'clock and had braved the heavy seas breaking on the sands to rescue some of the seamen. It was a great hazard for the gallant sailors and for the men they were rescuing and twelve seamen had been drowned in these operations before the Cromer boat arrived. Most of the *Taara*'s crew had already been saved.

Henry Blogg needed no round-table conference to decide his course of action. He made straight for the *Oxshott* as her need seemed most desperate for all that was showing was the funnel, upper deck and two masts and the sea was lashing them. The rest of the vessel was already under water. As the lifeboat got closer and there was no sign of life, Blogg concluded that they were too late to do anything and so moved round to the next ship, not fifty yards from the *Oxshott*. He was just considering how to tackle this one when some one spotted from the new angle sixteen men roped together behind the funnel of the almost-drowned *Oxshott*. Henry Blogg saw at once that of the two crews those men were in deadlier peril. So he turned back.

There was no place to secure a line with the decks well under water and big seas sweeping over them. Then the coxswain noticed a wedge-shaped crack in the upper works of the *Oxshott*, close to the funnel. If he could get the bow of the lifeboat in there for long enough he could take the shipwrecked men off. It would mean running the lifeboat right on to the deck of the steamer and a false move or a sudden sea would mean disaster. If she stuck fast she would certainly perish even before the dying ship. It seemed too great a risk to take, but that meant abandoning sixteen men to their fate and Henry Blogg's mind did not work like that, so he drove the lifeboat straight at the submerged ship. At 'Slow ahead' he nosed over the very bulwarks and deck of the steamer, bristling with jagged obstructions and put the bow of the *H. F. Bailey* into that small opening at the first attempt. Billy Davies the bowman yelled, 'Come on, boys,' and one at a time the sixteen men got free from their lashings and, dodging the seas, ran for the lifeboat.

The waves washed the *H. F. Bailey* out of the crevice, again and again, but each time her coxswain doggedly drove her back, trying to hold the red, white and blue bows in the rough crack as gently as he could with his engines. It was like a man putting his head in the mouth of a lion. One by one the seamen were dragged hurriedly into the lifeboat, spilling on to the deck in a wet heap, but never more glad in their lives of such rough handling. The *H.F.Bailey*'s crew yelled encouragement, 'Now's your chance. Run, me hearty,' and 'Any more for the lighthouse?'

Then Billy Davies flung a grapnel that held and enabled them to steady the lifeboat, but even so the seas swirled and scoured around them. Twice the lifeboat bumped heavily on the ship beneath and the splintering shudder told the crew she had been damaged.

As the last man tumbled aboard the *H. F. Bailey* Henry Blogg yelled, 'Give her a kick, "Swank",' and in a flash his mechanic had reversed the engines and the propellers were drawing them from that perilous perch. The bowman paid out the rope as they reversed, then, using it as an anchor, they veered down to the *Gallois*. She was in better condition for she was above water. The coxswain, watching the seas from all directions, brought his boat alongside; there was no time for mooring to the ship: every minute was precious, for it might mean a life. The line from the *Oxshott* was a precarious anchorage and he therefore supplemented this by the use of his engines and held his boat alongside with her head to the seas, just as he had done on the *Mount Ida* service two years before. While he held his station, taut and anxious lest a sea catch him unawares, thirty-one men slid down ropes or jumped into the boat as she rose on the crest of a sea.

The crew of the *H. F. Bailey*, excited and heartened by what they had already done on the *Oxshott*, shouted advice and encouragement to the crew. One seaman missed his jump, or slipped in the act of jumping and fell into the sea. But the Cromer 'crabs' were prepared for such a mishap and as soon as he surfaced a rope was thrown to him and he was dragged on board. The last man was in and the *Gallois* rescue was complete. There were now forty-seven soaked and shivering but happy men in the lifeboat as well as the crew of ten and there was not enough room to work. So the coxswain swung round for a near-by destroyer.

While his last rescue was in progress a bottle of rum was being passed round among the men of the *Oxshott* and one of the life-boat-men shouted jokingly, knowing what the answer would be, 'Can't we have a drop, Henry?'

'No, you can't. You can have some chocolate if there's any left,' replied Blogg with a grin and his mind on bigger things.

When they got alongside the destroyer and while the rescued men were being carefully transferred because of the rough sea, the same man yelled to the sailors who had gathered to cheer and banter them, 'Got'na rum, mates? We're dry as dust down here.'

Within two minutes, from the deck above, small tots of ration-rum were lowered and when the last seaman was aboard the destroyer the lifeboat-men were wet inside as well as outside and in even better spirits than before. This job really was going like clockwork!

It was now midday and back at home, twenty miles away over the troubled waters, dinners were being dished up. The crew felt peckish themselves, but there was more work yet before they could enjoy a hot meal.

While the transferring of men and rum was in progress the *Harriot Dixon* arrived alongside. Henry Blogg then decided that Jack Davies, the second coxswain, should take command of her as he had helped in two rescues and knew the conditions on the sands. While he turned the *H. F. Bailey* for the *Deerwood*, Jack Davies took control and turned the *Harriot Dixon* for the *Taara*.

The *Deerwood* was in a similar plight to the *Oxshott* with only her bridge above the churning sea. The waves were swirling over the submerged decks and smashing against the bridge. Nineteen men had taken refuge there and every sea that swept the ship threatened to wash them away.

Here again, what had to be done must be done quickly. Without hesitation Henry Blogg took his already damaged boat over the decks and brought her alongside the bridge, holding her there with his engines – a combination of *Oxshott* and *Gallois* tactics. As the seas broke on the ship the wind carried the spray over them in a deluge of salt water, but the nineteen men left their insecure refuge and jumped and scrambled into the waiting boat. Then Henry Blogg backed off and looked round for the next job.

He saw the *Aberhill* lying with her back broken and rapidly disintegrating and headed for her. When he got round to the lee side, however, he saw that the Great Yarmouth and Gorleston boat *Louise Stephens* was already there and taking off her crew.

The Yarmouth boat had great difficulty in getting alongside because of the surf around the broken ship, but she tied up to the *Aberhill* and took off twenty-three men.

Henry Blogg went on to the fifth ship, the *Taara*, also lying with a broken spine in a swirl of crosscurrents. He found the *Harriot Dixon* already `on the job' and Jack Davies was emulating the tactics of his coxswain by keeping bows to wind and sea and using his engines to lie alongside the wreck. Eight seamen jumped to safety.

Turning from the *Taara* to the last ship, the *Paddy Hendly*, Henry Blogg saw over a score of men crouched on the doomed vessel. This ship, like three of the others, had her back broken with the terrible strain imposed by the sands once they get a ship in their grip. The enormous power the sands bring to bear on a stranded ship is incredible.

Meanwhile, from the decks of the destroyers *Wolsey* and *Vimiera*, watching but not daring to get closer, the Navy noted with admiration the courage and skill of Cromer's coxswain. Vice-Admiral Sir John Cunningham, describing the rescue some months later at a ceremony in Cromer Regal Cinema, said, 'One of the ship's officers reported: "It was the finest bit of seamanship I have ever seen. It was a do-or-die attempt. They were a hundred per cent men, every man of that lifeboat crew."'

This time Henry Blogg brought his boat alongside the agonised *Paddy Hendly* and, keeping his head to wind and sea, he used his engines while twenty-two men jumped on the lifeboat deck. Then, weighted with fifty-one men, he swung away from the wreck – and almost into disaster! The tide had run so low and the lifeboat was so borne down with its load that twice the keel of the boat bumped heavily on the sands and then every one's heart missed a beat when it ran completely aground. What might have happened is not pleasant to think about. Once the sand began sucking at the boat and held it for the seas to smash, there would be a quick end. They watched, fascinated and helpless, as a big wave reared up on their port hand and swept towards them, but it lifted, instead of overwhelming the *H. F. Bailey*, and in another twenty yards they had reached deep water. It was a very nasty few minutes. The protecting hand of God was never more clearly displayed in Henry Blogg's adventurous life than at that moment. The merciful had indeed obtained mercy.

The work of rescue was over apart from landing the ship-wrecked men. The *Harriot Dixon* put her seamen aboard the destroyer and set course for Cromer; the *Louise Stephens* was already on her way to Yarmouth and at one o'clock Henry Blogg, with forty-one rescued men aboard, also headed for Yarmouth.

While throbbing southward Billy Davies the bowman espied the mast and bridge of a ship, probably the trawler *Agate*, which was also lost, above the water. They went to investigate, but there was no sign of life, so they carried on towards the Cockle Gat. A little later they met a destroyer and transferred the forty-one men. Then the captain of the destroyer asked Henry Blogg to go to HMS *Arkwright*, a distant trawler, as there were two dead bodies to bring ashore. The lifeboat did this, and carried on past Scroby Sands to Yarmouth, arriving about 5 p.m. The dead men were taken to a mortuary and the Cromer crew went to get food and hot baths.

Before Henry Blogg had a meal he arranged for the repair of the *H. F. Bailey*. It was found the sturdy boat had three holes in the port bow, twenty feet of port-fender ripped off, the bow-pudding and the stem torn off and its bolts, driven through eight inches of deadwood, had pierced several air-cases inside the hull. It was severe punishment, but she had been forced twice over flooded decks, bumped twice on the sands with a heavy load and she had run aground. The wonder was not that it was so much but that she had come through at all.

It was also learned at Yarmouth that the *Foresters Centenary*, of

Sheringham, and the *Michael Stephens*, of Lowestoft, had been out to the sands only to find the six wrecked ships deserted and the rescue work completed.

The *Louise Stephens* landed twenty-three men at Yarmouth, the *Harriot Dixon* had rescued eight and the *H. F. Bailey* eighty-eight. Altogether 119 men had been saved by the lifeboats.

There was a delightful sequel to this service when awards were presented by Vice-Admiral Sir John Cunningham KCB at Cromer. There was a packed audience in the Regal Cinema and the crew had already assembled in the hall when they were suddenly called out on a service. It was most inconvenient at that moment, but shipwrecks, like fires, rarely conform to a convenient schedule. It could not be helped. The lifeboat must go out. The meeting started and a little later H. A. Mitchell, chairman of the UDC, announced, 'I have just been informed that the call has been cancelled and we shall see our friends back in a short time.'

Some minutes later there was a commotion in the foyer and Henry Blogg and the Cromer crew trooped into the hall in their sea-boots. The clumping and chafing of the boots was just the touch of reality the audience needed to stir its imagination. There was a storm of cheering as the men took their seats at the front of the hall.

Henry Blogg received the second bar to his Gold Medal and also the British Empire Medal, Jack Davies got a Silver Medal, as did coxswain Charles Johnson, of Yarmouth. Several other Cromer men received the Bronze Medal.

The commander-in-chief, Nore, sent a message of congratulation on the 'Superb seamanship and courage displayed.' And while the congratulations showered in upon Cromer's crew, and the salvage officer, underwriters and courts of inquiry were busy the Haisborough Sands finished their terrible meal. When the wind died and the August sun shone at last from a serene sky, the sea made no sound upon the sands except where the little waves lapped and caressed the twisted sides of six total wrecks, a grim reminder that the tragedy and heroism of that wild August 6 morning were not just a fevered dream.

After the drama of the attempted rescue the previous day, and a night wondering if they would see the dawn, English Trader *crewman William Hickson still had the presence of mind to take this photograph of Henry Blogg's lifeboat as it approached his vessel.*

190

14

The *English Trader*

SOME TIME after the *Mount Ida* rescue the Cromer crew were using a reserve lifeboat, which had a very different motion in the water from their own boat. They rescued a crew from an unlighted ship a long way north of Cromer, with seas very short and sharp, and when Henry Blogg was talking to his solicitor about it Henry Murrell asked, 'Did the men tell you how it happened?'

'No, they didn't say anything.'

'Then, what did you talk about coming home?'

'Nothing.'

'Nothing! Were they ill, then?' asked the lawyer.

'Yes.'

'What was the matter with them?'

'They were seasick.'

'What! Sailors seasick?'

'Yes,' replied Henry Blogg, 'and you needn't sound so surprised – we all were.' And the coxswain suddenly began to shake inwardly with laughter at the thought of seamen and lifeboatmen hanging over the side of the lifeboat.

The crew were undoubtedly pleased when they got their own boat back and it is part of the wise policy of the RNLI to give the men a voice regarding the boat they must man. The Institution is not ruled by theorists but considers the coxswain's opinion and begrudges neither money nor thought in design and construction to give brave men the greatest confidence in their boats. But that does not remove the danger of being capsized or overwhelmed, for that risk is always there. The lifeboat must go into the very places that should be scrupulously avoided; the places where tides race and currents clash; and when the weather is in no holiday mood. Henry Blogg once said, 'I have been a seaman all my life and forty-five years of it have been spent as a lifeboatman. From that experience it is impossible to guarantee any boat against disaster. It does not matter what type of boat it is, you cannot ensure against accidents. All depends upon the force of the storm and the judgement of the crew.'

So, although Britain's fleet of 156 lifeboats is the finest in the world, the spectre of sudden disaster remains. Along the coast of Norfolk men and women remember the Caister lifeboat disaster of 1901, when the boat capsized in the surf, pinning her crew of twelve under her, and how old James Haylett and his son rushed into the sea and dragged three men out. They also talk of the Wells disaster of 1880 when ten men perished; and in 1941 a similar disaster almost befell the Cromer boat. Henry Blogg said later, 'How the boat righted herself I shall never understand. It must have been the hand of Providence.' As it was, five men, including the sixty-five-year-old coxswain, were washed into the sea and one more went overboard but hung on to the guard-rail and clambered back on board. The rest of the crew on the deck flung themselves down and the sea washed over them.

It happened on Sunday morning, October 26, 1941. The eight o'clock news was just beginning when Cromer coastguard called Henry Blogg and told him Yarmouth naval base had asked for a lifeboat to go to the aid of the *English Trader*, which had grounded on Hammond Knoll, a nasty sandbank where the depth of water changes from sixteen fathoms to four feet in a few yards. This sandbank, lying twenty-two miles east of Cromer, almost joins the serpent-like Haisborough Sands.

Henry Blogg accepted the responsibility for launching, as during the war Major E. P. Hansell, the secretary, was serving in the Forces, and within fifteen minutes the *H. F. Bailey* was tussling with a full gale from the north-north-east – an uncomfortable quarter at Cromer. Jimmy Davies described it in his diary as a 'terrible north-east gale'. There were heavy squalls of hail, which reduced visibility to a few yards while they lasted; there was rain and sleet and the sea was rough – altogether it was 'lifeboat weather'.

By ten o'clock they had passed the North Haisbro' buoy in order to clear the Haisborough Sands and then veered southeast. With this alteration of course the following seas were so rough that one of the crew stood by with the drogue ready in case of need.

They reached the Knoll about 11.30 and found the *English Trader* in her death throes. The entire hull was almost under water and the seas were sweeping her from end to end. Henry Blogg however, in his fifty years of service, had seen many ships similarly doomed and knew that his problem was the riot of seas that surrounded the wreck.

Sandbanks can be a boon, for they provide some shelter in storms by breaking the force of the waves. Many vessels anchor and ride out the gale in Yarmouth Roads, letting the Scroby Sands serve as a breakwater. When that has been said there is nothing else good about them. They certainly confront a lifeboat coxswain with grave problems as the behaviour of the seas on the sands is unpredictable. During a storm great masses of water, set in motion by wind and tide while moving freely through perhaps ten fathoms or more, are suddenly obstructed by a sandbank and forced into the shallows. They heave up and break out in all directions, making a confusion of tremendous currents and great seas.

Henry Blogg said this was the most appalling problem he ever had to face. They were not true-running seas. On the weather side they were racing along the ship's flanks like crazed animals. At times they ran from both directions along the hull and, meeting amidships, went up like a mine explosion. Some reached mast-height and then fell in a turmoil of hundreds of tons of water on the ship.

When considering that statement one must remember Henry Blogg's veracity. He would not exaggerate conditions. Early in his career his lawyer urged him in the witness-box to say the seas were 'rough'. It was a salvage case and the claim hinged on that; but Henry Blogg would not. His lawyer grew annoyed and said, 'Surely you would agree it was a rough sea?' A slow smile spread over Henry Blogg's face and then he said, 'Well, perhaps you would call it rough, but I wouldn't.'

He got a lecture from his lawyer afterwards, but that did not worry him.

Henry Davies said that while they were there he saw the spray from these great seas going right over the masts. His brother Jimmy described them as 'terrific seas'.

The crew of the *English Trader*, who then numbered forty-four as five had been washed overboard and drowned before the lifeboat arrived, were crowded for shelter along the side of the chart-room, away from the biting wind. But they could not evade the masses of icy salt water that were flung over the whole ship.

To add to the difficulty of rescue, the sea, like a mighty plunderer, had broken open the hatches and was scouring he cargo out of the holds. The surrounding water was a jumble of floating cases and barrels, which were being tossed about by the waves like toys. Moreover, as overweight, the ship's derricks had broken free and were swinging with the roll of the ship, like flails that would have crushed the lifeboat. Altogether, it looked absolutely hopeless. The *English Trader* was apparently beyond human aid.

There was shelter of a kind on the lee side but, even so, the internecine strife of the ocean made it impossible to get alongside. Henry Blogg told E. 'Boy Primo' Allen to signal the bedraggled survivors that he must wait for slack water – the period between the tides when the flow of water is slowed – which would occur at 4 p.m. and might last an hour or so.

Then they stood off into rough but saner waters to bide their time. But just after one o'clock, with the tide dropping appreciably, the coxswain thought he might move in. The line-throwing

William Hickson took this photograph of the English Trader *as Cromer lifeboat took him and his fellow crewmen to safety.*

gun was held in readiness by signalman Allen and the lifeboat-men came up close on the lee side, but the waves were still running at one another and going up in a great column. There was no getting alongside, for if the lifeboat took one of those seas on board anything could happen. It did seem a chance, however, to get a line to the ship, so the gun was fired, but the angle had to be so steep to reach the crew that the wind caught the projectile and blew it back between the lifeboat and the ship.

Once more they retired to wait a better opportunity. An hour passed. Not an idle hour but one in which the art of seamanship was fully employed keeping the lifeboat head-on to the seas. Then some of the younger members of the crew, growing a little impatient and with the dashing success of the convoy rescue fresh in mind, urged Henry Blogg to try again. But he was wily in the ways of the sea and said his chance had not yet come. So they hung on a little longer and then, when it seemed somewhat quieter near the *English Trader*, they pressed him again and he, thinking there was perhaps a chance, consented. It is the only time the strong-willed man gave way against his better judgement.

The *H. F. Bailey* moved towards the wreck. In her approach she had to turn broadside and was doing this when, in the coxswain's own words, 'We were trying to approach at half-speed and when still about 100 yards away a huge wall of water suddenly rose up on our port side, a shout "Look out," and before I could even give a half-turn to the wheel, I was lifted out of the boat just as though I had been a bit of cork. We were simply overwhelmed by the sheer weight of water. How the boat righted herself I shall never understand. It must indeed have been the hand of Providence. The boat must have been hit hardest abaft the fore cockpit. Had she been hit as hard along her whole length there would be no lifeboat crew in Cromer to-day.'

Huddled on the ship, the crew of the *English Trader* saw the lifeboat heel right over on her beam-ends until the keel came clear of the water. She hovered as though undecided whether to go completely over and then slowly righted herself. A few more inches would have meant utter disaster.

Besides Henry Blogg, who could not swim, Jack Davies, the second coxswain, R. C. Davies and his brother Henry Davies, 'Sid' Harrison and E. W. Allen all went overboard. R. C. Davies managed to hang on to the guard-rails and as the boat righted herself he hauled himself back on board.

After being carried through most of the broken water Henry Blogg opened his eyes and was much surprised to see the *H. F. Bailey* had regained her balance. Henry Davies felt the guard-rail under him as he was caught by the sea but did not grab it. In a flash he thought, 'The boat is going right over; if I grab this rail I shall be covered with it.'

There was a terrific sensation of cold as he was caught by the icy sea, then he found himself with his head above water. His kapok lifebelt kept his head up. Choking and retching with the water he had swallowed, he could not see the lifeboat. He was certain she had gone right under. Then he found himself against 'Sid' Harrison. They caught hold of each other involuntarily, then, realising that would not do, they released their hold.

Henry Davies said, 'This is a bad end, Sid.' Then added, 'Have you got your boots off?'

'Yes,' panted 'Sid' Harrison, 'I lost mine when I came over. Have you?'

'No,' gulped Henry, suddenly realising he was still cumbered, 'I've still got mine on,' and began thrusting with the toe of one sea-boot against the heel of the other to get rid of his boots. He struggled for three or four minutes and thought he would never be free of them, but with several sharp kicks he at last succeeded. He felt more buoyant immediately, but the cold seemed unbearable. It seemed to be eating right into him.

'Sid' Harrison was just saying something to him when a big wave lifted them high and parted them.

There was still no sign of either the *English Trader* or the lifeboat and he felt convinced the lifeboat had sunk. Struggle as he might, the sea swept over him and he felt his lungs were bursting. He came to the surface spluttering and choking and a sensation of despair swept over him. There was no point in trying to keep afloat. This brutal green sea would just torture him, filling his lungs with salt water and driving the last of his breath from him. Help could not reach him now. His body was numb and unresponsive, a jumbled, half-formed prayer went through his mind. Then a big sea caught and raised him high and there across the turmoil of the seas was the *English Trader* and, not fifty yards away, the *H. F. Bailey*. Someone saw him and before he slid into a deep trough of the waves he knew they were coming for him.

Meanwhile W. H. Davies had picked himself up and, although dazed and winded, took the helm. The engines were still running, so he called 'full astern'. Seeing Henry Blogg and his father Jack Davies in the water close by, he steered for them. Then someone remembered an aircraft dinghy that was stowed in the canopy. They got it out and flung it to Henry Blogg and he clung to it while they got the second coxswain on board. It was an incredibly difficult job to get the men into the boat. Apart from the weight of their sodden clothes, with sea-boots and oilskins, their kapok-filled lifebelts projected from their chests and caught under the deep bulge of the boat's fender. Moreover, the rescuers had had most of the breath knocked out of them by the weight of water that hit the lifeboat. 'Jack' said, 'When I got on board I put two fingers on the back of my tongue and got rid of some of the seawater.' When they got Henry Blogg on board he could hardly stand, but made his way, bent almost double, to the wheel. He clung on to the cabin for a few minutes while he got his wind and then recovering somewhat he took over and steered to where Henry Davies was floating. After a few minutes' search 'Sid' Harrison was found and also pulled aboard. E. Allen was farthest from the boat and when they neared him he was unconscious. The crew were so exhausted that they had to call the mechanic from the engines to get 'Boy Primo' Allen into the lifeboat. He had been twenty-five minutes in the water. They chafed and rubbed him; he revived and sat up and started pulling on his mittens. Then he spoke a few words and dropped back. They lifted him, and laid him under the for'ard canopy, and continued to apply artificial respiration, and chafed his hands and face, in an endeavour to revive him.

Henry Blogg felt so weak he had difficulty in turning the wheel. It was an ordeal for a man of sixty-five. Moreover, the boat was not responding either to engine or wheel as she should have done, and it was found some light ropes had been washed overboard with that big sea, and were wound round the propellers. All hope of doing any more for the shipwrecked men was out of the question. It was 3 p.m., they had been out seven hours and were all-in. It was decided to make straight for Yarmouth.

Helped by wind and tide, they made a good speed even with the fouled propellers and tried en route to contact Yarmouth naval base by radio-telephone, asking for a doctor and ambulance to be ready at the quay. But they could get no reply. However, their message was picked up by the Great Yarmouth boat, which was already on her way to the *English Trader,* and she relayed their message.

When the *H. F. Bailey* arrived at 6 p.m. there were both doctor and ambulance – but signalman Allen was dead. Some of the other members of the crew had suffered so much from exposure and exhaustion that they had to be helped out of the boat.

A sense of deep grief weighed upon them. 'Boy Primo' was the first death in their lifeboat history. He had served nearly forty years in their boats. 'He was a good-living loveable man,' said Henry Davies. 'He gave all his leisure to St John Ambulance work and the lifeboat.'

Before Henry Blogg would rest or take food himself he helped his mechanics to refuel the boat and get her ready for a return to the wreck at first light. There is no greater example of dogged refusal to be beaten. They were going back. They would save those forty-four men, and the life that had been sacrificed would not have been in vain.

Meanwhile the *Louise Stephens* of Great Yarmouth had left just before midday for that perilous Hammond Knoll. She had nearly twenty miles of heavy seas with a strong northerly gale to face, and the tide stream also against her. Her speed was little over a fast walking pace. She got to the sandbank shortly after the Cromer boat left, so the shipwrecked men saw the bows of one boat replace the stern of the other within a matter of a few minutes. But neither boat saw the other in the big seas.

Coxswain Johnson tried five times in two hours while it was slack water to get alongside the wreck. He did get a line aboard but it parted while they were hauling it up, and the boat was swept away.

The *English Trader's* crew, who had seen the mishap to the *H. F. Bailey,* watched apprehensively these renewed attempts, afraid lest a similar fate befall the *Louise Stephens* as she tried to get alongside. In the end the captain of the wrecked ship did a noble thing; he drew the lifeboat-men's attention by a shrill whistle and then waved them away. They wanted to be rescued as badly as anyone, but they felt like a bait luring these brave lifeboatmen into the snare of the terrible sands.

There was now no other course for the Yarmouth boat but to return home. The sea had won both rounds!

Back at Cromer, as the hours passed, a sense of foreboding greater than the usual anxiety grew among the relatives of the crew. Mrs Henry Davies, who had seen the boat go off at 8 a.m. that Sunday morning, felt strangely disturbed. At dinner-time the sense of something being amiss increased until, when it was nearly half-past two, a choking feeling came over her and she felt she could bear it no longer. She left the house and her two children and hurried to a neighbour saying, 'There is something wrong. I know there is.' Her neighbour was equally worried and they both went round to see Ann Blogg. She had heard nothing. She rang the coastguard but he could not tell them anything. They sat round the fire talking for an hour. Other women came. They rang the coastguard again. This time he had a message. The boat had wirelessed Yarmouth: 'Making for Yarmouth. Have ambulance ready at quay.' That did not seem out of the ordinary to them as they thought the ambulance was wanted for one of the men they had rescued.

But after six o'clock Ann heard Henry on the telephone. His voice sounded shaky and strained as he told her what had happened and how they had lost 'Boy Primo'. He said a car was coming to Yarmouth with dry clothes for the men and bringing another man for the crew. Ann passed on this message to the other women present and it was arranged for someone to see Mrs Allen straight away and break the grievous news.

The car took boots, socks, sou'westers, underclothes and jerseys. Later that evening Mrs Henry Davies got a parcel of wet clothes, delivered by the car, which had returned from Yarmouth. She was surprised to find among the soaked clothes her husband's watch and even more surprised to find it had stopped at 2.28 – the time she had been overpowered by the feeling that something was wrong and the time he had been washed overboard.

The saddened, worn-out men of the *H. F. Bailey* were given

hot baths and food at the Shipwrecked Mariners' Home and given some dry clothes. The crew of the *Louise Stephens* got in to Yarmouth about 9 p.m. They had had a hazardous journey with no lights and the heavy seas, but by going close inshore had picked up the outline of the land and followed the coast down. The crew were so wet and cold that coxswain Johnson decided not to refuel until the next morning and told the crew to reassemble at 5.30 a.m.

Henry Blogg had not gone to bed. He telephoned coxswain Johnson and discussed arrangements for the next day. On hearing of the Yarmouth boat's five attempts, Henry Blogg told him that any boat that got alongside that ship had accomplished a fine feat of seamanship. He said he was going to try again about 4 a.m. but coxswain Johnson said he would wait for daylight. The admiral in charge of the naval depot had told Henry Blogg that the boat was not to leave Yarmouth without his permission.

Round three of this fight with the North Sea began at 3:30 a.m. the next morning. Henry Blogg was up and had already got weather reports from the naval base and Cromer. Both agreed there was an improvement, but it was 'nothing to write home about'. In the cold and the dark the Cromer crew assembled, still rubbing the sleep out of their eyes. They looked weary. There was none of the usual banter but a subdued grimness. Nor was there a grouse that Henry Blogg had got them up again after such a brief rest. Like him, they were going to see this thing through. At 4.15 a.m. Henry Blogg asked the naval duty officer to arrange for the boom to be opened. He did not ask permission or inform the admiral of his intending departure, but he tried to contact coxswain Johnson by telephone to tell him he was just going out. As he could not do so he asked the operator to give the message as soon as he could.

That little touch of courtesy to another coxswain, and the 'blind eye' to the admiral's orders, was typical of Henry Blogg. It was another 'Nelson touch'.

At 4.40 a.m. the man of sixty-five who had been washed overboard and had been ten hours at sea yesterday with little or no sleep, was taking his boat through darkness and rough weather towards the Yarmouth Roads. He had three hours of darkness and anxious navigation ahead and a difficult boat to manage, for the ropes had not been cleared from the propellers. There were also many memories of a lost comrade that were too deep for speech. The lifeboat throbbed north-eastward with hardly a word spoken or order given, her churned wake spreading and losing itself in the darkness and the wet oilies of her crew shining in the deck-lights.

So they hobbled along with wind and spray catching and lashing them and exactly twenty-four hours after they had set out from Cromer they reached the wreck the second time. The joy of the shipwrecked men seeing them come out of the grey dawn light brought a faint cheer over the water.

Their persistence in the face of grim adversity shamed even the weather, for when they neared the sands the light was breaking and the wind that had lashed them unmercifully for so long veered to the north-west and then suddenly dropped. The sea also moderated. Carefully, but with comparatively little difficulty, they took the lifeboat alongside on the *English Trader*'s lee. A rope was thrown and the *H. F. Bailey* moored. Within thirty minutes the forty-four survivors were taken off. They had spent a bitter fear-ridden night on their sea-swept decks. They had believed the lifeboat would return with daylight but had wondered if they could hold out that long.

Three hours later the hungry, exhausted men of the *English Trader* were being helped ashore at Yarmouth quay. The third and final round had been won by the Cromer lifeboat.

The *Louise Stephens* had put out at 6.30 that morning and reached the Knoll only to find the work of rescue had been completed.

Henry Blogg was awarded the third service clasp to the Silver Medal and the rest of his crew were awarded either the Bronze Medal or clasp. Coxswain Charles Johnson was also awarded the Bronze Medal. The Institution awarded the widow of Edward Allen a pension, as though he had been in the Navy and killed in action.

15

Closing Years

THE SECOND World War brought more danger and more work to all the lifeboats. It also brought more opportunities for heroic service. This applied particularly on the East Coast, where from the ranks of Britain's magnificent lifeboat-men two figures emerged – coxswain Robert Cross of the Humber and coxswain Henry Blogg of Cromer. They were both past normal retiring age when the War began and although Robert Cross handed over the helm in 1944 at the age of sixty-seven, Henry Blogg saw the War out in spite of being nearly seventy.

Behind Norfolk's curved coastline was a great concentration of airfields, mostly bomber, with large numbers of aircraft going and coming, sometimes singly like summer bees to a hive, sometimes in swarms. Many a flak-riddled bomber limped home across the North Sea only to come down 'in the drink' off Cromer. The lifeboat went out on innumerable air-sea rescue jobs, looking for an aircraft or elusive dinghy in the waste of waters. It was usually a fruitless search, for the aircraft had gone straight in or the pilot had already been picked up. They did, however, save many lives – a complete crew of six or just a lone 'tail-end Charlie'. Once they found a plane and searched diligently for the pilot, until some one recognised the aircraft as a pilotless 'Queen Bee'. They towed the machine almost to the shore before it sank. Another `aircraft' turned out to be a barrage balloon from a convoy and this also was taken in tow. The Cromer men disliked leaving anything lying about and would probably have had a go at bringing in a disabled battleship!

There were many calls to find the shocked survivors of mined or torpedoed ships adrift in small boats in rough seas; to take salvage officers to wrecks and supplies to tugs on salvage work. All these demands were extra to the normal calls from storm, fire and stranding. And to extra work was added extra danger from floating mines, quick-striking E-boats and aerial attack on shore and ship. When the tally was made at the end of the war Cromer station had the finest record in the country, with 155 launches and 448 lives saved. In January 1940, while bringing in the crew of the 7000-ton SS *Traviata*, which had been mined and sunk, an enemy aeroplane circled the lifeboat as if to attack, but turned away to bomb and gun a near-by trawler. Henry Blogg immediately boarded the trawler to give help and found her captain bleeding profusely from bullet-wounds, the deck a shambles and the engines out of action. The lifeboat-men gave first-aid to the skipper and then towed his ship for three hours until the engines were going again.

The next day they rushed out to aid a light-vessel which had been bombed and machine-gunned by some ignorant (or inhuman) enemy pilots. There had been an excellent salvage job the previous month when the mined tanker *Dosinia* was found listing heavily. The *H. F. Bailey* took off her crew of fifty-one and then stood by for the rest of the night. At daybreak a floating mine was spotted right in the path of an oncoming convoy and the lifeboat went towards it and signalled the leading ships to alter course. After that diversion the *Dosinia*'s captain thought of beaching his ship, but made such satisfactory progress that he proceeded slowly northward with the lifeboat accompanying him to the Humber, where tugs took charge. The crew was put back on the tanker and the lifeboat stood by until morning and then returned to Cromer, arriving at 5 p.m. after forty hours at sea. The *Dosinia*'s captain said that without the lifeboat's help he could not have saved the ship.

Apart from the convoy – and *English Trader* – rescues there were several heavy jobs during the war. One of particular interest was to the 9500-ton SS *Meriones*, of Liverpool, which was stranded on Haisborough Sands on January 22, 1941. There were 101 men and two racehorses on board. Enemy Dorniers found the helpless ship with naval and civil tugs trying to get her off the sands and in three attacks dropped twenty-three bombs, but only wounded one man.

Henry Blogg was asked to go at once to Yarmouth and accompany another tug to the vessel and advise on the salvage operations. When he arrived at Yarmouth he was asked by a recently promoted salvage officer how much his fee would be. Henry Blogg did not expect this and said, 'Oh, never mind about that. Let's get on with the job.'

But the officer was going by the book and said he wanted to know just what he was committed to.

So Henry Blogg said he did not want any fee and that he only wanted to 'see the ship saved'.

This was not good enough and the official was just proposing a fee of ten guineas a day when the Harbourmaster intervened to say that precious time was being wasted.

So they went by tug to the stranded vessel with no settlement. After another aircraft attack on the ship the Cromer lifeboat was also sent for and arrived at 3 p.m. on January 25 to find her coxswain already on the scene.

The sky grew pewter-coloured, wind and sea increased, flooding the crew's quarters and breaking loose the horse-boxes. It was decided to abandon ship. Taking a grave risk in the darkness, the *H. F. Bailey* tried to tie up alongside the vessel, but although four-inch ropes were used they parted. Eventually, with six-inch and nine-inch ropes, she was secured and in spite of great danger took off fifty-three men and transferred them to a tug. She returned and took off forty more, then the thick ropes broke, so these men were also transferred to the tug and at the third attempt she took off eight more, including the injured man. The horses were shot. The lifeboat then made for Yarmouth, but the light-buoys were extinguished and in the darkness, with rain and sleet squalls, Henry Blogg was afraid of running on to sandbanks near the Cockle Gat, where heavy seas were breaking. Although it meant waiting over five hours in bitter cold, the coxswain would not risk proceeding, but anchored until daylight. The salvage officer was doing some inaudible grumbling. In the dawn Henry Blogg identified Winterton Steeple on the shore and fixed his position. He carried on to Yarmouth and landed the rescued men, including the young salvage officer.

The last-named had not been ashore long before he told the Harbourmaster that he did not think much of the Cromer coxswain.

'Why not?' was the blunt question, for the Harbourmaster had already formed his own opinion of this young man's capabilities.

'Because he couldn't find his way here in the dark. We had to anchor half the night in the freezing cold, waiting for daylight.'

'When did the naval tugs leave the wreck?'

'Oh, they left some hours before we did.'

'Did they indeed! Well, you ought to know that they haven't come in yet!' said the Harbourmaster with asperity.

There was such a heavy swell for three days that the lifeboat could not be brought home and during this time enemy aircraft again bombed the *Meriones* and set her on fire.

Jimmy Davies recorded in his diary: 'A very rough trip but one of the best jobs we have done.'

There was a sharp scuffle between E-boats and a convoy escort in March 1942. HMS *Vortigern* was sunk by torpedoes, but not before she had destroyed three and damaged two E-boats. Two ships of the convoy were also sunk ten miles north of Cromer and although the *H. F. Bailey* searched four hours for survivors she found only dead bodies.

On December 7, 1944, Henry Blogg gave a proof of his staying-power, which for length of service exceeded the five-launch spell eight years earlier. The old man of sixty-eight was at sea continuously for sixty hours. This was the service to the *Samnethy*, a Liberty ship stranded on Hammond Knoll. The *H. F. Bailey* was launched about midday and throbbed over a calm sea to the Knoll, where she stood by while four naval tugs tried to move the ship. The weather kept fine until midnight on December 8 when the lifeboat, which had remained handy, had to move into deeper water. A gale, with sleet and intense cold, then made operations so difficult that Henry Blogg warned the naval salvage officer on December 9 that if the crew were to be taken off it must be in day-light. It was not until afternoon, however, that he was allowed to begin operations. He got alongside and moored, but the ropes parted in the heavy seas and fouled the lifeboat propellers. A special knife is provided for such an emergency and with this the propellers were freed. She tied up again. The seas were lift-ing and dropping her fifteen feet, but she took off thirty-five men and transferred them to a tug and went back for seventeen more. Having got these off she made for Gorleston, reaching harbour on the morning of December 10. The tugs freed the *Samnethy* from the Knoll the same day.

For six years there were big jobs and little jobs, fine rescues and futile searches. They all came in the run of duty. And there were no 'office hours' for the lifeboat. They could be wanted at any or for all of the twenty-four hours of the day and often it seemed that most of the calls came in the small hours of the morning or when the weather was in a rip-roaring temper.

Apart from 155 launches there were another fifty or more false alarms, during which Henry Blogg watched weather and tide for hours. There would be many telephone calls before he learned that the little fishing-boats could make the shore without lifeboat assistance, or the dinghy had been confirmed as empty.

If we can turn all these 'alerts' into telephone calls, weigh the responsibility for life-saving over a wide area of busy sea-high-way, add the normal demands of fishing and living and then allow for what life has already drained in forty years of heroic exertions, we can easily understand why Henry Blogg had to see his doctor about heart trouble. In addition to the strain of con-stant lifeboat services, Henry Blogg had what was for him the stiff ordeal in March 1942 of making a broadcast appeal for the lifeboat in the 'Week's Good Cause' in the BBC Home Service. There were 6800 replies which brought in over £5000. One gift, not very large and yet, perhaps, the largest of all, touched Henry Blogg's heart. The accompanying letter read:

> I am sending my pocket-money to you this week so that you can help God to keep Bobby and John safe and all the other children's Daddies safe.
>
> Love,
>
> ALLEN

He also sat for his portrait by T. C. Dugdale RA. This was hung in the Royal Academy that year and now hangs in Lifeboat House. The artist has captured not only the character of the man but of the sea off Cromer, so that an eminent naval officer, seeing the portrait, said, 'That's Henry Blogg and that's the North Sea.'

Another portrait by William Dring was shown in the National Gallery in the autumn of 1942.

In March 1946 the Cromer branch discussed the question of Henry Blogg's retirement. The great coxswain was seventy years old, ten years over the retiring age. He had held the position of coxswain for thirty-seven years. In exceptional circumstances the retiring age could be extended beyond sixty-five and Henry Blogg felt he would like to continue for another year, so in view of his unrivalled record of service to humanity it was agreed that he should do so.

In 1947, therefore, Henry Blogg took off his kapok lifebelt marked 'COX' for the last time and his nephew Henry (named after him) Davies was elected coxswain of the *Henry Blogg* and his brother 'Jimmy' coxswain of No. 2, with Lewis 'Tuna' Harrison acting as second coxswain for both boats.

Only those who have laid down a task that has dominated their lives for over half a century can imagine how Henry Blogg felt when he left that meeting. His step was lighter, for the burden of responsibility and always being 'on call' was now on younger

Admiral of the Fleet Sir John Cunningham makes one of several awards to Henry Blogg to mark his retirement as cox'n.

shoulders. But there was also a sense of loss, as though something that was part of him had suddenly been taken away. Yet Henry Blogg had the satisfaction of knowing that he had given to the Cromer lifeboat station a tradition that would always inspire those who took their place in the crew. Henry Davies said, when talking about Henry Blogg's most comprehensive will, 'He left me more than money.' He left to all of us a legacy – the example of putting service before self.

When the maroons sounded he would go to the slipway and, standing apart, watch with narrowed blue eyes peering across the tumbling, spray-obscured sea as the lifeboat disappeared – without him. He who for thirty-eight years had taken her out on almost every launch now watched as the *Henry Blogg* went out on her mercy-mission without Henry Blogg. The beautiful boat was away on her errand and he whose only crime was age must await her return on the shore.

Although the coxswain released his grip of the helm, he did not step out of the lifeboat service in the mind of the public, for his record was such that he had become a legend. The daring, the self-sacrifice and skill of the service were personified in this quiet man. His qualities had kindled pride and admiration all over the world, for he had not risen in one supreme moment to some peak of heroism but through over fifty years he had shown that courage, judgement and endurance were the very essence of the man. He had helped to save 873 lives.

It was on January 4, 1948, that Henry Blogg went on his last service in a lifeboat – this time not as the coxswain but as No. 7 of the crew and Henry Davies took the helm. It was a call to aid the steam trawler *Balmoral*, which had been fishing in the North Sea and had run aground on the Haisborough Sands.

Her flares were seen, but when the lifeboat *Henry Blogg* reached her the trawler was abandoned. She had, however, refloated herself and was drifting into deeper water, so Henry Davies put five men on board and went in search of the crew. They found them in a small boat and one of them was ill. They took them on board the lifeboat and towed their boat to the trawler, which was then in ten fathoms of water. The crew were put back and after thoroughly examining their vessel they continued on their original course. The *Henry Blogg* accompanied them to the light-vessel and then went on to Cromer where the sick man was taken to hospital.

It was August 19 that year, after the Institution had awarded Henry Blogg an annuity, that Admiral of the Fleet Sir John Cunningham came to Cromer to name the new lifeboat the *Henry Blogg*. This boat was the first to have the steering wheel amidships instead of aft and Henry Blogg had reported favourably on the change after being asked to test it. 'It is the best boat I have ever handled or seen,' he said. During the ceremony the Admiral said, 'To all of you I would say that Henry Blogg's record is quite unequalled in the whole 124 years of the lifeboat service. We in the Admiralty have a very lively appreciation of the consummate seamanship which Henry Blogg exhibited on so many occasions.'

The old man felt very proud that day, for he not only received a copy of his portrait painted by T. C. Dugdale RA and a certificate of service, but from friends and admirers he accepted a cheque and an illuminated address. In the leather-bound volume

Two Henry Bloggs: the man and the lifeboat carrying his name.

there were cameos of crabs, Cromer church, Henry Blogg's beach-hut and a distress signal. The address read:

> In the seventy-two years that you have lived in Cromer and particularly during the fifty-three years that you have served the RNLI, you have by your deeds and example brought great credit upon the town, which is proud to call you citizen, and upon the lifeboat service.

The first name of a long list of subscribers was that of HRH the Duke of Edinburgh.

Without a garden and a hobby there was an emptiness in his retirement, for life for him had always been so full. He had now so much time he did not know what to do with it. He never went to the theatre except when in London to receive an award. He went a few times to the local cinema with his wife and once he went to see *Old Mother Riley* and thoroughly enjoyed it. The fact was that Henry Blogg had lived for the lifeboat service. Although he could have gone away for a day or a week if he had arranged for a deputy, he rarely did so. He never had a holiday, although the change would undoubtedly have done him good. He had been reared when uninterrupted work was the rule for fishermen and holidays the prerogative of the well to do. Later, when he could have broken that rule, he did not want to do so. His work was his life and his life was his work.

Even in his reading he first looked for items concerned with lifeboats. Not that he was a reading man, but he occasionally read a book if a friend recommended it. After absorbing news of lifeboats he studied football and cricket. He took a keen interest in both and it was there that his reticence ended. During the test matches Henry Blogg was always 'routing' for England. Had he lived to hear the exciting series of 1954 he would have spent many a tense hour over his radio. (He looked forward to television but never had it.) He loved to watch a game of football, rarely missing a home match. Although holding no official position, Henry Blogg was a stalwart Cromer supporter by his presence, if not always by his comments! If he would not criticise

Henry and Ann Blogg at home in Swallow Cottage in their later years.

fellow lifeboat-men or politicians, he was an arch football-critic. Perhaps he saved it up. The man who stood next to him on a football ground heard 'Bad centre,' 'Oh, weak shot,' 'Poor tackle,' and similar epithets. If a player could sort out Henry Blogg's comments in the welter of advice offered to most players he only heard something uncomplimentary. If the coxswain was silent that player knew he was doing all right. Although not a player himself, he was a good judge of the game and while wanting Cromer to win he never begrudged the better team the victory.

In addition to supporting Cromer he also followed Norwich City and the Arsenal, Alex James and the Comptons being his idols. He had, however, a wide knowledge of other teams and knew not only the current league positions but the history of most leading players.

In 1950 Ann Blogg became seriously ill and needed almost constant attention. The district-nurse called regularly and relatives – particularly Mrs Jimmy Davies who lived next door –

were a great help during this time of stress. When Ann sufficiently recovered Henry Blogg would take her in a wheelchair
down to the beach. But the improvement was only temporary. A
masseur called regularly to try to assist her to use her limbs more
freely, but later that year a stroke stilled the tired heart. She was
buried beside Queenie.

When Henry Blogg came back to his empty house in Corner
Street he was a lonely man. His life, for all its honours and great
achievements, had not been one of sunshine. The shadow of tragedy had fallen many times across his path. He had lost his only
son as a baby and his beloved Queenie in her twenties and now
the wife who had stood by him through the stress of so many
crises. The Cromer lass he had married when an unknown young
man had been his partner for forty-nine years. She had been
intensely proud of him, treasuring his medals and little souvenirs of epic services and doing everything she could for him. She,
who would not even let him set a cup on the table, had to leave
him with his medals and his souvenirs to fend for himself.

Gradually and with slower step, Henry Blogg adjusted himself to his loneliness. He brought his bed downstairs and tried to
teach himself to do the little tasks of the home that had always
been so scrupulously dealt with by other hands. Just how much
he had to learn was illustrated when some friends came to see
him and left some table jellies for him to make up himself. On
their next visit they asked how he liked them. Henry Blogg
replied, 'Oh, they went down all right. I soon drank them!' But
his needs were few, for he lived simply and life had lost its zest.
He would go to his hut on the promenade and sit in the sunshine
listening to the drumming of the sea. He would talk to customers
and friends and come home in the evening to prepare the little
food he wanted, sit at his desk to write up his books and then go
to bed.

The cosy evenings when Charlie Cox would drop in to make
up a foursome of whist or 'Heigh Ho Jack' with Ann and Queenie
and himself belonged to the past. He, alone, was left. But sometimes he would go to the little rocket-house gardens near the

old boat-house and sit there with some cronies, gazing over the wide sea, talking of other years. The old men who had been boys when he was a boy would talk of the Goldsmiths' School, School-master Hudson, the *Fernebo* and the *Sepoy*. Henry Blogg would feel young again as he looked down at the beach where these dramas had been enacted and relived the setbacks and the final triumphs of those famous rescues. Then he would look at the summer sea, blue and calm, and reflect; he had beaten it then, but now he had grown old, his heart was weak, his step slow and his life very lonely. Yet the sea had not aged or changed – it had outlasted him.

As a young man Henry Blogg had always referred respect-fully to the older fishermen as 'those fine old gentlemen'. Now, he kept free from the fault that sometimes goes with age – he never criticised the younger generation. Part of the first and only public speech he made, at the end of his career, consisted of two sentences – 'Cromer always has had good boats and good crews. And it always will.' There was no pining for the good old days before modern youth let the side down.

In 1952 he was the guest of Commander J. E. Jowett of HMS *Crossbow*, a destroyer lying anchored off the town. When the ex-coxswain went aboard from a relief lifeboat the Navy gave him a great welcome that really did his heart good.

Henry Blogg had not the worry about money that many old people have to face, for by his lifetime of frugal habits, by labo-rious fishing and his share in the beach business, as well as a number of useful money awards from salvage operations, he had saved several thousand pounds. Money was his servant, how-ever, not his master. When a rescued Dutchman offered him money for what he had done, Henry Blogg replied, 'It's not that what I'm here for. Spend it on telling your wife that you are safely landed.'

Nor did he aim at publicity or mere medal collecting. 'The sat-isfaction of having done your best is better than any reward,' was his comment once, on being congratulated.

It was in June 1953 that the old ex-coxswain received the

The visit of Henry Blogg (ex-coxswain), H. T. Davies (coxswain of No. 1 lifeboat) and J. W. Davies (coxswain of No. 2 lifeboat) to Cdr. J. E. Jowett on the destroyer HMS Crossbow, *1952.*

blow from which he never recovered. The crab-boat *Boy Jimmy*, manned by the brothers 'Jimmy' and Frank Davies, his nephews and 'Ted' Bussey their mate, was just coming in from fishing, when fifty yards from the shore it suddenly capsized within sight of all on the beach. The men were all experienced fishermen, the boat was perfectly seaworthy and the sea was not rough. The boat was held in the grip of an 'undertow,' or undercurrent, caused by some unusual feature of the beach, which makes a strong 'flow back' of water to the sea, perhaps five to ten yards wide. The backward flow retards the incoming wave, which sometimes builds up into a mass of water that must break. The boat too is held back by this current against the oncoming wave. Such a wave caught the *Boy Jimmy* and completely swamped it. The little boat went straight down. Its crew could all swim well but with their heavy sea-gear and possibly knocked out by the weight of water, they had no chance. The wife of one of the men was standing on the cliff waiting for the boat. She saw the boat capsize and just heard a faint cry for help come over the water. That was all. Such tragedies, although rare, can happen to any fisherman. As the coroner said at the inquest, 'It is a hazard of fishing.'

There is a price on fish that can never be shown on the ticket.

Only nine years before Charlie Cox and Gilbert Mayes, both members of the lifeboat crew for over thirty years, were crab-fishing in the *White Heather* with seven other boats when a wave capsized the boat. The lifeboat was launched immediately and they found the body of Charlie Cox, but neither Gilbert Mayes nor the boat was ever found.

You can never wholly trust the sea. Even when it wears a smiling face its heart is cold and hard. That treacherous trait keeps man from giving his heart as unreservedly to the sea as to the good earth.

Henry Blogg was on the beach and saw the *Boy Jimmy* capsize. Although he had a weak heart he rushed down the beach and helped to launch the only crab-boat there. The effort was too much for the old man and even as the boat got away he collapsed a few feet from the water's edge. They took him home and the doctor examined him, but there was little that he could do. Blogg seemed stunned and lost all desire for food and drink. He never recovered from the shock of that disaster.

That cruel wave had flung a shadow across the whole town. In many homes the blow seemed unbearable. One young widow was left with four children, the youngest three years old; a mother had lost two sons; two men had lost two brothers and a small community of fishermen was decimated. One little girl was told by another child in the street that her father had been drowned. She ran home sobbing. The young mind sought reassurance and she cried incessantly to her distraught mother, 'My Daddy isn't in the water, is he?' 'Where is my Daddy?' 'I want my Daddy.' There was no answer even in a mother's arms.

Henry Blogg rallied to give courage to the young widows and to help with the fatherless children. From his own experience of sorrow he gave some comfort in this time of need. Little three-year-old Elizabeth Davies would climb on his knee to chatter and then snuggle her fair head against his blue jersey, seeking a security she had lost. Although his own bodily strength declined, the old man became a source of moral strength to the bereaved.

But apart from feeling the sorrow of the mourning families, Henry Blogg had a great affection for his nephews and 'Ted', and the last year of his life was clouded by personal grief caused by that tragedy.

16

Farewell

HENRY BLOGG'S heart got steadily worse, slowing down all his activities. He did not give up work completely, but although he was at his usual spot at the bottom of the 'Doctor's Steps' he could not keep to his former routine. Very often the steep slope of the east gangway proved too much for him and he was glad to get a lift in a van from the beach up to Church Street. He continued to look after himself in Swallow Cottage until the end of May 1954, although Mrs Jimmy Davies did more than ever for him. Then, one lovely day when the woods about Cromer were in full leaf and the blue sea reflected a fair sky, he complained of sharp head pains and when Dr Donald Vaughan came and examined him he diagnosed severe shingles.

For a fortnight the lonely veteran of the sea was nursed night and day by his relatives and the town nurse in his own home. He refused to be moved to the house of any of his nephews and the suggestion of removal to the Cromer Hospital found even less favourable consideration. Not unnaturally, he did not want to leave his own home for a strange bed.

Night after night Henry Davies sat up with him, going to his fishing in the daytime. Mrs J. Davies gave every minute she could spare from her own children. Other members of the family helped all they could. The old man was never left alone and everything that love and nursing could do to ease his great pain was done. He, who had responded so readily to the needs of others, found a ready response to his own need.

The shingles affected his face and eyes and in the end the doctor prevailed on him to go to the hospital. He was carefully moved and placed in a private ward. There, in spite of every possible attention, he grew weaker and was still in much pain. Relatives and friends visited him, noted the change and knew the ship was nearing the harbour. He also seemed to know that his voyage was almost complete and was satisfied. The long watches through fair weather and foul had been faithfully kept; the ties had long since gone and the tired blue eyes longed for sleep. He gradually slipped from the pain-tormented realm of consciousness into a merciful semi-coma. Although unable to speak, he sometimes gripped the hand of the visitor with a pressure that betokened recognition.

The end of the long, gallant voyage came on Sunday June 13, 1954. Henry Davies went to see him and the old man seemed much better, for he gripped his hand and spoke to him. His nephew left the hospital at 7.30 p.m., feeling more cheerful as to his uncle's condition. When he arrived home at 10 p.m. he was met with the news that Henry Blogg was dead. For a time he could not believe it. He felt there must have been a mistake. But there was no mistake; the heart that had withstood the strain of so many epic struggles with the sea had ceased to beat. The man who had courted danger for sixty years on the storm-tossed sea had died in his bed.

There was no last message, unless it was found in Tennyson's immortal words:

> Sunset and evening star,
>> And one clear call for me!
> And may there be no moaning of the bar,
>> When I put out to sea,
> But such a tide as moving seems asleep,
>> Too full for sound and foam,
> When that which drew from out the boundless deep
>> Turns again home.

At 5 p.m. on Wednesday June 16, the body of the seaman was taken to the parish church of SS. Peter and Paul, the church that had kept him in its protective shadow all his life and that has stood through the years, like a watchman on the walls, looking out over the encroaching water of the North Sea. In the red-carpeted chancel, before the altar with its gold-embroidered cloth, the coffin was placed, draped in the flag of the RNLI. There, in that place of hallowed memories, where the people of Cromer have worshipped since 1387, where he had stood fifty-two years before at his marriage, the greatest of Cromer's sons was laid like a king in state. On the magnificent tower high above the town and the sea the flag was lowered to half mast. It flowed landward as the sea winds stirred it. From the flagpole in the churchyard and others in the town, flags were similarly flown, dipped to salute a man beloved and admired.

From that tower in other years a light had shone to guide mariners, but the light had long since gone out. The coffin in the chancel was a reminder to the hundreds of people who filed past that summer's evening that another light had gone out – Henry Blogg would sail the seas no more.

On Thursday 1400 people, gathered from all over the county, packed the church to pay homage to Henry Blogg. Outside, another thousand waited in the churchyard and formed a square five-deep around the low church-wall. Nothing like this had happened around this coast before. It was unforgettable. The splendid church, with its weathered flints and storm-worn masonry, towered protectively above the mourners standing in sorrow and silent homage. It seemed not a mere building but an old, understanding friend. From within came the low pealing of the organ leading the congregation in the hymn 'Oh God, our help in ages past'. Between the verses and above the sounds of a strangely subdued town, came the low, continuous rumble of the sea – the sea that had fed Blogg and fought Blogg and now seemed to murmur its last mighty tribute to him.

There was no 'dim religious light' inside the great church, for the lofty aisle windows did not hinder the June daylight, but showed up the red-and-black tiled floor, the blue pew-mats and the cream walls. Graceful pillars carried the eye upward to the dark hammer-beam roof, where winged angels hovered high above the heads of the people. Through the stained glass that edged the aisle windows came shafts of blue, red and green light. It was a solemn but not a colourless scene.

The relatives of the lifeboat-man stood in the chancel. Before them was the draped coffin and beyond it the altar with its brass crucifix and candlesticks and above them the multi-coloured east window.

At the choir entrance a magnificent wreath shaped like an anchor bore the card of the RNLI committee of management, another shaped like a helm was from the officers of the Cromer branch. Resting against the coffin itself was the wreath from Blogg's crew; from the men who had served, suffered and succoured with him for half a lifetime. Every available seat in the church was occupied. The atmosphere was not one of grief, but rather of proud thanksgiving. The deceased had not been struck down in the pride of youth, leaving a broken-hearted family and unfinished life-work; Henry Blogg had come through to a ripe age and his bundle of life was tied up and labelled. The people had gathered not so much in sorrow that he had died, but to be glad that he had lived.

After the Ven. Robert Meiklejohn, Archdeacon of Norwich, had read the lesson the vicar of Cromer, Rev. D. T. Dick, paid a tribute that might have sounded extravagant, for he called Henry Blogg 'Cromer's greatest son'. But the hundreds gathered there knew this was no mere funeral compliment. It was the truth. The deeds and character of Henry Blogg had gone round the world and coupled with his name was their town – it was Henry Blogg of Cromer'.

As the choir led the singing of 'Rock of Ages', blue-jerseyed fishermen from all round the storm-racked coast of Norfolk, coastguards and shop girls, bar-tenders, leaders of the county's life and workers on land and sea swelled the singing.

Viscount Templewood, president of the Cromer branch, faced the silent congregation and in quiet words summed up the life of the man they mourned. 'He was,' Lord Templewood said, 'the very embodiment of the spirit of courage of the north Nor-folk fishermen. Thanks to his leadership the Cromer lifeboat has become the most famous of all lifeboats. He was a national char-acter.'

The service ended with the hymn 'Eternal Father, strong to save', and as they sang many fishermen and townsmen thought of 'the restless sea' that at that moment was fretting its limits not fifty yards away. When they reached the end of that verse they looked at the coffin and in their mind's eye saw Henry Blogg clad in stiff yellow oilies and lifebelt, standing at his wheel as the boat plunged into the angry waves to answer the call of those 'in peril on the sea'.

'From rock and tempest, fire and foe, protect them whereso'er they go' – that no longer applied to Henry Blogg. He had passed beyond the power of the sea and the storm. But there were bare-headed, blue-jerseyed men there who to-morrow must go down to the sea to fish or man the lifeboat and who needed to be pro-tected while wresting a living or a life from the sea.

The grand hymn ended. The benediction was pronounced. The congregation remained standing and while the choir sang the Nunc Dimittis the flag-draped coffin was lifted on to the shoulders of four Norfolk coxswains: Henry West, of Sheringham; W. Cox, of Wells; J. Brown, of Caister; and B. Beavers, of Gorleston. It was then borne down the centre aisle, over the tombstones of Cromer's former townsmen now sleeping in the nave, over the worn flagstones of the porch and out into the June sunlight. As the coffin-bearers emerged from the church two loud reports startled the mourners and in the sky over the sea two puffs of smoke appeared. The maroons had been sounded! They were the signals that had so often brought Blogg and his crew from work or from bed to face the rigour and danger of the North Sea. It was a vivid symbol, a fitting tribute to a great man.

The coffin was placed in the hearse and the cortege formed. The fishermen of Cromer and Sheringham – the Wests, Craskes, Davies, Peggs, Coopers, Middletons and Prices – under the direction of Lewis 'Tuna' Harrison, coxswain of Cromer No. 2 boat, led the cortege. They were dressed in their traditional suits of navy blue, with strong boots, heavy woollen jerseys and carrying their cloth caps. There were many very young men and many white heads conspicuous against the dark suits. The latter were the men who had known Blogg since his youth. They had played with him and worked with him. They had shared with him hundreds of dangerous launches. They had pulled at the oars against mountainous seas until the blood had pounded in their ears with the strain; they had been hungry, half-frozen and drenched; they had defied death and the fury of the sea time without number when he had led them. They had brought hope and mercy and life to hundreds of their fellow men because he had inspired them. They had climbed farther and higher than they believed they could because he had struggled ahead and beckoned them on. His daring and his seamanship had been their boast and however dark the hour – they had trusted their lives to his leadership. They could pay no higher tribute. Now they were accompanying their great coxswain on his last journey. What memories crowded their minds as they walked to the new cemetery! Was it surprising that many a broad red hand brushed away a sudden tear as the thoughts of other years came back like a flood-tide? They knew that in the street, on the promenade and on the cliff-top they would never again see the erect familiar figure of 'Old Henry'. The hearse, the family mourners and fifteen official cars followed the band of fishermen. Mr Kelly Harrison, bowman of the lifeboat, carried Blogg's twelve decorations on a black-velvet cushion. A lorry carried a hundred wreaths – a riot of summer's colour in the midst of navy blue and black.

The procession formed and moved past the west door of the church, along High Street and New Street; past the spot where Henry Blogg was born and within a few yards of the cliff-top, where he had stood so many times scanning the sky and gauging the weather. The route was deeply lined by people who watched silently as the cortege turned into Prince of Wales Road and inland along the Holt Road.

On the outskirts of the town the fishermen fell into two ranks on either side of the road, allowing the hearse and mourners to

The funeral cortège, with the pier and lifeboat house in the background.

pass on their long journey to the new cemetery, nearly two miles out of town. Then they got into a coach and, by making a detour, arrived at the gates before the procession and lined the main entrance.

There, on high ground, in one of the loveliest parts of Norfolk, overlooking the heath and wood and the distant sea, they laid Henry Blogg. The seaman was home from the sea.

They left him there and the man who never had a garden was now covered by costly flowers. Away from the sea's moaning and the gulls' screaming, he lies buried beside his wife Ann and his daughter Queenie. A simple, grey, mottled kerb and head-stone enclose the spot bearing the short name, the strong name, the unforgettable name – Henry Blogg.

From all over the world, from the famous and the unknown, from seamen and landsmen came high tributes to the Cromer fisherman. But perhaps the simplest acknowledgement of his qualities came from one of his crew who said that day: 'Had he been in the Navy he would have been an admiral; in the Army he would have been a general. Whatever he chose, he would have been "the guv'nor". He was that type of man.'

Whether Henry Blogg chose the sea or the sea chose him, we do not know. He certainly chose the lifeboat service and in that service he became the 'Greatest of the Lifeboat-men!'

Perhaps the simple sincere words of a Dutchman whom Henry Blogg saved from a wreck are his best epitaph:

> I shall keep this noble man in my memory till the end of my days and by doing so I shall also pay a tribute to the longshore-men and fishermen in general of the East Coast.

Index